The Project Management Guide
to Planning and Implementing
System Installations,
Conversions and Mergers

BANK
SYSTEMS
MANAGEMENT

Kent S. Belasco

A BankLine Publication

PROBUS PUBLISHING COMPANY
Chicago, Illinois
Cambridge, England

A Bankline Publication

ISBN 1-55738-380-4

Printed in the United States of America

BB

CTV/BJS
1 2 3 4 5 6 7 8 9 0

Probus books are available at quantity discounts when purchased for business, educational, or sales promotional use. For more information, please call the Director, Corporate/Institutional Sales at (800) 998-4644, or write:

Director, Corporate/Institutional Sales
Probus Publishing Company
1925 N. Clybourn Avenue
Chicago, IL 60614
PHONE (800) 998-4644   FAX (312) 868-6250

For Paul

Contents

v

Contents

Introduction

How often has it transpired when a new system was purchased that cost overruns began occurring, as well as missed deadlines? Has it ever so happened in a bank that the approximate timeframe communicated failed to occur, and was instead extended considerably, or with indefinite targets? When projects are completed, is there a strong sense of comfort that all of the tasks have been completed?

Unfortunately, there is usually a high degree of discomfort when confronted with these issues. Why is this? From a banking perspective, the reason is that the people who recommended the idea or concepts to be implemented aren't usually skilled in the disciplines necessary to see a project through. The ingredient most often missing is the *discipline* found in the science of project management. Project management and implementation are not functions generally found in the job descriptions of most financial institution executives. Banks borrow and lend money; that is their principal function. Implementing projects and the like are primarily the province of systems, engineering, and construction. So why spend time on it?

Regardless of the industry, everyone needs project management skills. As a matter of fact, every professional manager leaving school should have had training in project management. The reason for this is that the discipline and skills gained in managing projects are invaluable in today's dynamic work world. In particular, with technology rapidly changing, change no longer is a one-time event but rather a way of life. Because of this change, the ability to direct tasks and functions towards a defined end is the only way a manager can effectively manage resources, time and costs.

The purpose of this book is to focus on these questions and outline methods that can be used by bank employees to ultimately reduce or eliminate the concerns associated with these questions. For financial institutions as service providers, technology is vital to continued growth and success. Without the necessary systems and hardware, banks cannot survive in today's competitive arena. Because of technology needs, there will always be conversions, mergers, transitions, upgrades, and various forms of automation. This is now becoming the norm.

With this moving target, how do bank managers ensure success? More importantly, how is a project completed on a timely basis, to capitalize on an opportunity or to coordinate with other planned events?

Bank Systems Management: The Project Management Guide to Planning and Implementing System Installations, Conversions and Mergers is designed as a guide for educating bank managers on the disciplines required to coordinate and manage projects. It is not intended as preparation for an engineering career, but rather sound training for any manager. Today, project management is—or should be—necessary training for any student of management. The skills developed by applying this book's principles can enable readers to accomplish a large volume of tasks and projects within defined timelines and with limited resources.

In the banking industry, regulations change on short notice. The government, unfortunately, does not provide much latitude in implementation time or whether a project should be undertaken. When deadlines are short and are imposed from without, project management skills are a must in order to meet deadlines.

Project management is a well-defined discipline. The concepts presented in this book are not intended to be revolutionary or cutting edge. That intent is to outline how project management can and should be applied to the needs of banks—not for engineers or scientists. The skills and concepts discussed are those used in an actual bank environment and are written for bank professionals and nontechnical professionals. Using the approaches as they are intended will practically guarantee positive results. The approach will also eliminate the sense of loss of control and other gnawing feelings of runaway costs, uncertainty, and frustration. The skills are management essentials and enable the professional to multiply, severalfold, his or her individual productivity. *Bank Systems Management* is a handbook and reference guide designed for bankers which can be used repeatedly for the implementation of telephone systems, microcomputer systems, mergers, acquisitions, new software, or any process requiring multiple steps. The goal of the book is "getting it done" planned, budgeted, and implemented.

1

Organization and Management of Bank Projects

BANK PROJECT MANAGEMENT DEFINED

What exactly is project management, and why is it needed? For financial institutions, in the 1990s, it is a much-needed discipline and process that is vital to organizational and system planning. In order to define project management it is necessary first to understand what a project is. One definition I have found to be rather descriptive is: "A project is a one-time job that has defined starting and ending dates, a clearly stated objective, or scope of work to be performed, a predefined budget, and usually a temporary organization that is dismantled once the project is complete."[1]

Essentially, *project management* is an organized or structured approach for managing a variety of independent and interdependent events and activities leading toward a common outcome. The objectives of the approach are to

♦ Complete planned activities in accordance with a stated timeframe

♦ Deliver the completed project or product on time, with minimal slippage

♦ Manage the costs of the process so as to ensure attainment or reduction of budgetary projections

♦ Monitor the results of the process to ensure that the purpose and benefits of the system or project have been accomplished

Although these objectives appear to be straightforward, or even simplistic statements, meeting these objectives when literally hundreds of activities and multiple people are involved is truly a challenge. The basic objectives indicated are akin to the basics of management in general. One might argue that any manager who possesses the basic skills of a manager could be an effective project manager. In some cases this is true, however, the difference lies in the breadth and type of management involved. Depending on the scope of a project, the project manager may be responsible for managing the results of a number of professionals over whom he or she has no legitimate authority. In other words, direct-line managers have a benefit over project managers in that the people they manage report to them, are evaluated by them, and are responsible to them. In a project environment, this is not the case. Project team members generally report to others and, in some cases, may even outrank the project manager. The skills required, therefore, must be finely honed in order for the project effort to be successful. More will be discussed on the specific skills of project managers later in this chapter.

For banks and financial institutions, the purpose or need for these skills revolves around the current trends in the industry. In today's world, the rapid advance of technology has created an ever-changing environment, necessitating project management abilities. Technology no longer is a revolutionary concept. Financial institutions today cannot survive without technology. In general, the entire service industry itself must use technology in order to remain competitive in the marketplace. Those organizations that have not computerized or taken advantage of the technologies available today will not be able to function profitably. Because of this necessity, there is a continual need for analyzing/evaluating software and vendors, implementing new equipment, converting old equipment, and managing multiple tasks and events. These functions have become the norm in the industry rather than the exception, and as such, have dictated a need for an organized approach to managing them.

PITFALLS

Considering the state of flux and fast-paced technological evolution, this management phenomenon is
inevitable. Organizations that lack the approach or
skills to manage technological transitions effectively
can fall as far behind in the marketplace as if they
didn't use the technology at all. Inadequate installations and implementations can be costly ventures. The
price tag on rework, project delays, or budget overages
can literally eradicate any proposed savings or opportunity originally considered by the project. This truly
is a problem, but one that nevertheless occurs quite
regularly.

Banks can avoid such pitfalls through the commitment their managements make to the process of
implementation and activation. If organizations are
serious about spending the money to obtain the software, hardware, or other new equipment, they should
equally commit the funds necessary to see to a smooth
and timely transition. Again, this is money well spent:
Project management pays for itself in ensuring
planned and known events, rather than surprises.

Unfortunately, today, many projects and other
engagements taken on are not simple and require the
systematic execution of a multitude of tasks with a
high degree of precision. In the scientific and engineering community this situation is standard. For
banks, however, this is not standard operating procedure. Unlike the scientific and engineering worlds, any
projects initiated by banks involve much more than
the execution of specific systems and technological

tasks. The projects also involve the communication and assimilation of the concepts for end user and customer alike. In this sense, this book focuses on the social side of project management as well as its technical and operational sides.

AREAS FOR APPLICATION

Unlike many publications on the market today, this book is written for bankers and financial institution executives by a banker. Its focus is on a practical methodology for using specific concepts for the effective management of a variety of projects and events that can and do occur in the financial services arena. The concepts outlined in this book have been used and are in use today with proven results. The emphasis is not only on the fundamental aspects of bank project management but, more specifically, on its application in real-life bank situations. To that end the latter part of this book is devoted to specific case study examples and how the concepts of project management are employed.

Financial institutions generate many applications for which these skills can be applied. This list describes the needs most typically seen for project management in banking, revolving around a number of common areas.

♦ *Mergers and conversions.* Today, bank mergers and conversions to new data processing systems are commonplace. With changing state and national legislation, this approach has become a legitimate way to grow quickly as well as capture market share without major developmental effort. Many times opportunities presented require rather quick response in order to bid on targeted acquisition candidates. Once managers make the decision to bid and are successful, the real job becomes assimilation. Given the traumatic nature of acquisitions on personnel, the assimilation process can be fraught with problems and can severely impact or retard the planned opportunities considered in the decision to acquire.

Converting a newly acquired bank to the existing data processing system involves more than just a change of system (data processing). The conversion involves changes in procedure, policy, communication, image, and numerous other factors, some of which may have nothing to do with information technology. Nevertheless, there are myriad items to consider in converting a bank into another organization. These items must not only be identified but also effectively managed.

Another phenomenon exists besides conversions: bank mergers. Many organizations are continuing to consolidate, legally, to take advantage of cost opportunities that arise as a result of economies of scale. Mergers are slightly different than conversions and require a different set of tasks or functions to consider. This too, is not merely relegated to system issues, but can clearly involve a variety of "soft" issues that nevertheless must be identified and managed.

♦ *Platform Automation.* Platform automation is another relatively new occurrence in the banking world. As its title implies, automation involves systems, generally from a computer standpoint. The automation of the platform is a pervasive and ambitious undertaking that involves virtually all areas of the bank in one way or another. Banks, like other industries, are striving to provide their sales staff with more effective tools in order to obtain a competitive edge in the marketplace. The automation of the platform involves a variety of tasks and functions for the completion of the entire project. This may include software, computer hardware and peripherals, network equipment, installation, training, preventive maintenance, and so on. The coordination of these functions requires a well-defined process and skills in order to achieve the stated objectives.

♦ *Hardware Installations:* Today bank employees rely heavily on information technology in the form of various pieces of hardware. These can and do include teller terminals, personal computers, telephones, networks, data circuits, and various other types of equipment. In many cases installations usually relate to multiple installations rather than single units. In all cases there are many tasks and functions that must be considered in the process.

♦ *Miscellaneous Implementations*: Many times banks may have a need to coordinate the implementation of consultant recommendations, or the effective management of a multitude of tasks leading toward a final outcome. These variety of management tasks involves coordinating training, implementing the latest regulations initiated by the government, or developing of a new product. All require organization and coordination, especially when deadlines are imposed.

♦ *Software Changes and Upgrades*: Banks cannot live without software of some sort—in most cases, mainframe processing. However, with the advent of end-user computing software purchases, upgrades and changes have put the process squarely in the lap of the banker. The growth of end-user computing through networked personal computers has elevated this need to new levels. Often, bank management purchases software without an organized process or approach—in other words, purchasing software simply because it appears to meet the need or is the least expensive. If the software package requires a considerable expenditure, outside consultants may be engaged to perform the analysis and ultimately perform the project management functions necessary to implement the software. Although this is an acceptable approach, it is a costly alternative that adds considerably to an already expensive package of software.

In this book the structure and guidelines are outlined to provide management with the options for completing projects with *internal* resources. As an alternative, the book organizes the tasks so that the financial institution can pick and choose which tasks internal staff can and would like to perform and which they prefer to contract out.

BENEFITS

Two of the primary benefits of project management skills are the assurance that all tasks are identified and completed, and also the provision of a definite psychological aid to the transition process. In almost all cases, the types of change events that necessitate project management skills represent major changes to the organization. As everyone by now knows, change is not easy. When it pervades the organization, the actual transition will be somewhat bumpy. The project management approaches, tools, and skills outlined in this book help to make the process much smoother. The reason this works is that if communication is conducted on a timely basis and everyone is made aware of the timeline for project completion, people can gradually come to accept the change as it methodically occurs through the project's stages. In other words, there is great psychological value in presenting a major change event to an organization early on, then sharing with everyone concerned the progress made on a regular basis leading toward the project's completion. In this way, abrupt change is avoided and staff members have time to adapt to whatever change will affect them. Time, then, becomes the transitory agent. If project management is used properly, the outcome is less cultural shock and greater acceptance with less disruption.

This benefit alone merits considerable attention. The sheer organization and method of project management can make the difference between chaos, non-acceptance, and assimilation. In this day and age of rapid or fast change, the financial institutions that will survive are those that can assimilate the fastest and move on to the next event. In other words, change is here to stay. It is probably the one thing that can be counted on in an uncertain industry (and world). Those who have the skills and organization to quickly take advantage of emerging or leading-edge technologies truly have an advantage competitively. However, merely using new and emerging technologies doesn't always provide the edge. The advantage is gained only by the ability to quickly assimilate the change and incorporate it into the organization's philosophy to obtain the desired results. The approaches and skills outlined in this book provide the means for assimilation—both the physical implementation and ultimate staff acceptance.

If the staff never comes to accept or adapt to the event causing the change—a merger, new software, automation of functions or whatever—the benefits originally projected will not be attained. Furthermore, this could cause the beginnings of the downfall of the organization in general.

UNDERSTANDING THE NATURE OF A PROJECT

Longevity: Is It a Project?

According to Webster the definition of a project is, "A planned or contemplated venture."[2] Generally speaking a project also connotes a temporary event or set of events with a defined beginning and end. In other words, it does not continue in perpetuity. For the purpose of this publication the focus will be on those ventures, temporary in nature, which relate to banks and financial institutions.

It should be understood that projects do end, although in some cases they may require a lengthy timeline. In other cases projects can and do grow into institutionalized functions. A project that sees the implementation of an end-user computing system, for example, will nevertheless end; however, what will remain is the ongoing management of the system. This is an important distinction. To clarify this, projects can be split into two types: terminal projects and developmental projects.

Terminal Projects. Terminal projects are ventures undertaken for the sole purpose of implementing a specific set of tasks and events. When they are completed, there is no residue. Generally, these types of projects include implementation of regulation updates and changes, conversions/mergers, and some equipment installations.

Developmental Projects. Developmental projects, on the other hand, can be characterized as leading to other projects or forerunners to new permanent functions or activities. In a sense, the project portion of these ventures is usually performed to "develop" something. Once it is developed, the next phase will require an implementation (another project) and, finally, this phase may lead directly into a defined or permanent function.

Both terminal and developmental projects are specific and can be identified by the characteristic that they will, in fact, end. In other words, termination is precisely the objective of a project: to complete the tasks within the timeframe stated, within cost constraints, and with the original purpose initially established.

Organizational Impact

Projects have a tendency to have a rather pervasive impact on the organization. Depending on the nature of the project, it can directly affect a variety of people. Thus, the overall effect on the organization must never be underestimated. If a project is organized and managed properly, as defined in this book, the process should literally become part of the normal work world. However, the results or the outcomes intended will undoubtedly change the behavior of one or more people. In this regard, project managers must take care to prepare the organization for the change, which will inevitably occur, by nature of the project process and its outcome as well.

Although the necessity of good communication is discussed more thoroughly later in the chapter, proper communication is an absolute must for the successful completion of a project. This type of communication is not only to senior management and project participants but to the bank as a whole or, at the very least, to the beneficiaries of the project outcome. Projects will require time away from the day-to-day job for project participants. Therefore, it is vital that managers understand, up front, that a commitment is necessary that may be to their detriment temporarily.

If the project is large or has a significant impact on the organization, project mode status can heighten the energy level within the organization. In other words, it changes the routine from "business as usual" to a sort of tentative state. This is both a positive climate and also a precarious climate in that, at its inception, most individuals will truly be energized with the concept, involvement, responsibilities and opportunity to be a part of an exciting venture. As time goes on, however, the regular day-to-day workload does not stop. This "double duty" adds to the overall responsibilities of the individuals involved, which can affect their energy and drive. Senior management must be sensitive to the double duty staff members are performing and ensure that the overall project coordinator can effectively assess and comprehend what adjustments may be required.

In short, projects affect organizations in many ways. It must never be taken for granted that a major project can be conducted from beginning to end without a sensitivity to its impact to the financial institution. Recognition alone is half the battle. The remainder rests with an astute eye for the changes that are occurring and a sensitivity to the commitment required.

ORIGINATION OF THE PROJECT

When is it necessary to apply the skills and process outlined in the book to complete a given set of tasks? When does the venture warrant such project stature? In short, what constitutes a project?

There unfortunately is no specific rule of thumb managers can apply to any venture to determine whether it necessitates project initiation. As a general rule, the discipline of project management is best suited to situations that involve the following:

- ♦ Three or more individuals responsible for completing the tasks

- ♦ Several tasks to be completed

- ♦ Tasks that must be completed over a period of time (at least one month)

- ♦ Tasks that are interdependent (one must be done before another)

- ♦ Tasks that must be performed at specified times in order to be successful

These rules provide the basis from which to determine whether it is necessary to formally designate a series of tasks as a project. Once "project status" has been invoked, the steps outlined in the remainder of this chapter will provide the background to get the process started. In most cases, however, when a bank launches a major program—product change, software enhancement, or hardware upgrade—it can be safely assumed that the program will qualify as a project.

Although this point may seem obvious, a word of caution is necessary. When new ventures are initiated, if they are not "formally" adopted by the organization as a project even though they qualify, the risk for mismanagement is greatest. Without formal identification as a "project," the organization of the tasks to be completed may be too "loose." Invariably, every project that I have been involved in, small or large, had surprises. The only barrier to chaos was the discipline that was invoked by nature of the project itself. In other words, although the process the project team endures may be tedious, mundane, or simply redundant, the process synthesizes the necessary ingredients for successful completion and coordination of project tasks. Managers cannot assume that tasks will get done without formal adoption of the project. This adoption of project status forces attention, discipline, and order to whatever the team will attempt to accomplish.

Once a complex series of tasks begins but remains unidentified as a project, many activities are put into motion requiring people to make independent assumptions and decisions that may—or may not—contribute to the whole. Once complex tasks start, it is difficult to stop or attempt to impose discipline later.

In short, the lack of structure wastes time and does not efficiently *and* effectively deal with the issues at hand: the attainment of the original goals.

It is important for the organization to understand that project management should be the modus operandi for any type of implementation, installation, or set of events that the bank elects to undertake. Project management should become the standard discipline, the skills of which are learned not only by project managers but also by all managers and professionals in the organization. When this discipline becomes the accepted norm or standard for the financial institution, the synergistic effect created will benefit the bank for years to come in improved efficiency, timeliness, and effectiveness of project handling.

PROJECT SCOPE

Once the project itself is defined and the need is recognized to invoke project status, project managers must define the scope. As previously stated, projects are temporary. As such they have specific starting and end points. This is the "window of time" in which the events and activities are carried out leading toward implementation. At the point of recognizing project status, it is important to formalize what the project will and will not do, that is, to create a scope statement.

The scope statement is a written understanding of the boundaries within which the project will remain. It specifies what will be affected, where changes will occur, and ultimately what will be accomplished. To a degree this statement contains the "orders" for the troops who will initiate the project.

The scope should be formally documented once the need for the project is recognized and approval has been given to proceed. The scope not only is communicated to the people involved—project manager and committee—but also to all affected managers in the financial institution. This is important as it will serve to narrow the world of possibilities and provide definition. Without it, it is left to interpretation as to what falls within the terrain of the project team and what does not. If this ambiguity occurs, delays will be experienced as people's conflicting notions are thrashed out, a lack of organization will result, and ultimate disarray will prevail. In short, the ambiguity is detrimental to the project.

The scope statement for any project should be formal and should be developed in accordance with the following structure:

1. Project title

2. Purpose or mission of the project (why)

3. Detailed/exact specification of the project outcome

4. Listing of departments that will be affected and how they will be affected

5. Benefits of the project

An example of this document is illustrated in Exhibit 1.1.

Exhibit 1.1 **Project Scope Document**

Project: Implementation of a Platform Automation System.

Purpose: To provide salespersons with immediate access to information in order to assist them in increasing sales and cross-sales of products.

Project Outcome: The installation of a personal computer on each salesperson's desk in addition to a laser printer. Each personal computer will be connected to a local area network. A sales support software package will be accessible on this system.

Benefit: Improved sales revenue. Increased sales ratio and increased net income.

Departments Affected:

Location	Department	How Affected
All	Personal Banking	Automate account opening, and sales information
Main	Operations	Eliminate the need for data input of new accounts

SUPPORT AND COMMITMENT

As with anything worth doing, it is certainly worth obtaining all the support necessary to guarantee a project's success. Whenever a project is undertaken, it generally will transcend the entire organization. Because of this, those individuals involved in the coordination of the project will communicate, facilitate, organize, and direct a wide variety of people, many of whom have no formal reporting relationship to one another. It is difficult enough to coordinate multiple activities, but when the expectations involve tasks that must be completed on a timely basis by people that cross reporting boundaries and that affect an even broader group, the opportunity for conflict is high. For this reason, obtaining the appropriate support and commitment by the senior executives as well as the managers of the people involved and/or affected is vital to its success.

Support and commitment, in this vernacular, is more than just giving approval. Support and commitment involves active communication by the bank's management of what will be involved, who will be involved, why it is undertaken, and what the effect will be to the individual. For this reason, formal kickoff meetings are highly recommended to set the stage for the events to follow. Chapter 3 discusses kickoff meetings in more detail.

Once it is understood in the organization that the project is fully endorsed by management at all levels, it is easier to conduct the day-to-day tasks of matrix management. All managers can then "buy into the process" and literally become a part of it. This owner-ship will greatly improve the odds for subsequent success.

ORGANIZING THE PROJECT

Once the project is defined and endorsed by the company, the project itself must take form. This involves assigning the appropriate professionals who will ultimately carry out the tasks and functions necessary for full completion. The organization of a project involves a selection process in two areas:

♦ The project manager

♦ The project committee

Each assignment requires careful analysis and evaluation in order to select proper individuals who can be instrumental in the overall implementation of the project.

Project Manager

The first decision management should make is the individual who will coordinate and direct the project from beginning to end. Next to the initial decision to proceed with the project, this is the most important decision involved in the project management process.

Skills/Traits. Selecting a project manager is not a simple task. It involves identifying an individual in the organization who possesses the following skills and traits:

♦ An implementer, results oriented, with an understanding of timeframes

♦ Well organized, capable of managing a number of items at once and maintaining an appropriate balance

♦ Detail oriented; one who can provide documents and records to chart progress

♦ Strong communicator; one who can command respect from a wide variety of people without legitimate authority

♦ Well positioned in the organization

♦ Good time management skills

♦ Willing to accept responsibility well

If this seems like the ideal manager, it should, because the skills of a project manager are those of any good manager: planning, organizing, controlling, and directing.[3] For project managers, however, it is necessary that some traits be enhanced. An individual who has been characterized as or frequently called on to get the job done is a likely candidate. These individuals are motivated by results and the challenge of meeting tough deadlines. It is highly likely that most organizations could easily develop a list of potential candidates that have this type of reputation. Beyond that, the screening process should focus on the specific traits and skills just identified. In other words, a bank could possess an energetic, implementer-type individual; however, he or she may be very disorganized and abrasive. This is not the ideal candidate.

The project manager must combine the aforementioned traits into one package, because of the diverse situations the project manager will face. This candidate will work closely with a wide variety of people as well as management, outside vendors, and others.

Reporting Relationship. The project manager should report directly to the initiator of the project. In many cases this could be the executive committee, board of directors, or other type of senior management committee rather than an individual. If this is the case, a regular reporting of progress will be required to this body of professionals.

Project managers can report to individuals and do not necessarily need to report to a CEO or board of directors. This depends on the size of the project and its impact on the organization as a whole. In other words, if the project will impact everyone in the organization, as with a new communications system (network, voice mail, telephones, and so on), a high-level reporting relationship is a must. This will help the project manager to gain organizational support and endorsement for the project.

If the project itself is limited in terms of its organizational impact and affects only one department or specific segment of the business, the reporting relationship may be only to the division manager of the group that is being affected. This reporting relationship does not have to be formal. It can be a matrix relationship, indicating that the project manager is responsible for reporting the progress, status, and implementation timeframes to the manager of the division. The formal reporting relationship of the project manager may be to another division. In this case, the evaluation of this individual would be based on how well he or she manages the project and communicates effectively with the manager and parties most affected.

Banks seldom have divisions that employ project managers as a defined position. This may only occur if the bank has its own Information Systems division and regularly implements a number of projects. In most cases, the role of project manager is extracurricular to the staff person's formal position and is used on a temporary basis, by nature of the projects themselves.

Roles and Function. So what does a project manager do? In terms of a job description, the role and responsibilities of a project manager are not much different than those of day-to-day department managers. The major difference is that the project manager is working within a short or defined span of time. In other words, the role is tactical rather than strategic, or long term. Therefore, the skills of the individual must be intensified, because there is usually little latitude in time to perform various tasks.

The formal role or responsibilities of the project manager are outlined in the job description shown in Exhibit 1.2. This can be used when designating employees for this type of position.

Selection. Once an understanding is gained as to what is required, selecting the project manager is relatively easy. A review of the management ranks

---

**Exhibit 1.2   The Responsibilities Section of a Typical Project
Manager Job Description**

RESPONSIBILITIES:

1. Selection and management of the project implementation team

   ♦ Assignment of project tasks and responsibilities to committee member

   ♦ Periodic monitoring of the progress of each committee member in accordance with target dates

   ♦ Matrix management of committee members to provide direction, assistance, and support in the execution of their duties

2. Development and management of project documentation and reporting

   ♦ Development and completion of the basic project plan, with periodic updates provided

   ♦ Development and maintenance of project timelines, to coincide with the project plans

   ♦ Development and maintenance of budgetary monitoring and reporting throughout the project life

   ♦ Maintenance of committee meeting documentation to provide track records of issues, concerns, status, and results during the project

---

**Exhibit 1.2   The Responsibilities Section of a Typical Project
Manager Job Description (continued)**

3. Chairperson and facilitator of the project committee
   meetings

   ♦ Chairing all project committee meetings and facilitating
     the flow of information at such meetings

4. Regular communication of project status to management
   and affected employees

   ♦ Development, provision of updates, and maintenance
     of management summary reports and bulletins to com-
     municate project status and results to senior manage-
     ment

   ♦ Provision and/or direction of the periodic communica-
     tion of issues to the employee (user) base that will be
     affected by the outcome of the project

5. Responsibility for the completion of the project within defined timeframes and within the designated budget

   ♦ Monitoring all costs to ensure adherence to predeter-
     mined budgets

6. Provision of coordination and management of all third-
   party vendors, consultants, or independent contractors
   used during the project

   ♦ Monitoring and management of all contracts and en-
     gagements required in the process

---

should reveal an individual who possesses the skills and other characteristics needed for the position.

Once the individual is identified, the manager of this person must be consulted to determine whether the manager and department can afford to be without the candidate's services for a defined period of time. The time commitment must be spelled out clearly to the candidate's manager. In most cases, project management requires a full-time commitment for the duration of the project. This point is extremely important, because if the manager does not fully understand the time commitment involved, he or she will continue to count on the candidate to perform specific tasks within the department. As a result, the project manager will be unclear as to which job is the priority. In this situation, both the project and the regular department duties will suffer, and the project manager will be unfairly held accountable.

Whoever said no person could serve two masters was absolutely correct. Project managers must be fully extracted from their mainstream duties in order to be successful. To do otherwise is not only ineffective but also an injustice to the project manager.

To summarize, the project manager is the most important person involved in the project. Care should be taken in selecting this individual based on the requirements and guidelines previously provided. The overall successful implementation of the project rests with this individual. In this respect, if the bank has approved the funds to proceed with the venture, it behooves the financial institution to give itself the greatest opportunity for success by taking this selection seriously.

Project Committee

The project committee represents the functional group that will not only perform many of the tasks involved but will also oversee the progress of the project. Similar to the project manager, the bank should exercise care in selecting these individuals in order to guarantee the project's ultimate success. The project manager is the individual who directly selects the committee members or has very strong input in each decision.

The committee itself must be an action-oriented group, capable of working together and focusing on the many activities and issues involved in the process.

Composition. The project committee is constituted of bank employees from various disciplines, which fall into two broad categories:

♦ Functional members

♦ Control members

Functional members are those professionals who will actively perform many of the tasks and functions necessary for project completion. These are employees who have specific knowledge of the tasks or are responsible for the aspect of the business that will be affected. This group forms the nucleus of the project team. They report directly to the project manager on a matrix basis and are accountable for the functions and tasks assigned to them in the project plan.

Control members, on the other hand, are usually not doers but rather overseers. They represent the control aspects of the bank and are there to provide guidance, direction, assistance, and implementation as it relates to specific policies, procedures, or regulations. Typically, these individuals are

- ♦ Auditor

- ♦ Systems analyst or programmer

- ♦ Compliance officer

- ♦ Training officer

- ♦ Communications officer

- ♦ Purchasing agent

- ♦ Operations staff

This is a generic listing of control members who would or should be used with any project, regardless of its purpose.

Roles and Responsibilities.The committee is the primary vehicle for action within the project. The roles and responsibilities of the two broad categories of members are defined here.

Functional members must be selected to perform the specific tasks outlined in the project plan. They are selected on the basis of their experience and knowledge in the area that must be accomplished. For example, if the project involves the installation of a new computer system, one of the primary team members would be the personal computer or end-user system manager. In addition to this, the department manager or managers who will be affected by this (from one or several locations) must be involved. They will be the actual individuals who will be responsible for implementing it in their respective departments. These are the users of the information or hardware for which the project was initially undertaken.

Control members represent the individuals responsible for the general functions of the bank; they are designated as committee members to ensure that specific procedures, policies, and regulations are adhered to, or at least built into the process.

- ♦ *Auditor:* An auditor is necessary to provide guidance during the building stage of new systems, products, and functions. They generally can highlight areas of concern in terms of separation of duties and other concerns that will affect the bank in general. Their presence provides valuable insight into areas that may be overlooked in the process and areas that may be subject to violation of policy from a bank examiner or regulator standpoint.

- ♦ *Systems analyst or programmer:* In most cases, a project will affect some aspect of the data processing system in some way. Because of this, it is advisable that a representative from the bank's in-house data processing department or a representative from a third-party EDP vendor, if the bank uses a service bureau relationship, attend. Their primary role

is to provide input on any system-related concern relative to compatibility, interfaces, system or network architecture, or other concerns
relative to the project.

♦ *Compliance officer:* Similar to the auditor, the
compliance officer will monitor areas of regula-
tory concern that may not be immediately evident to the project manager or functional
project committee members. Their role is to
raise issues that may be of concern with respect to the myriad of regulations affecting
banks today. These regulations are generally
too voluminous and steeped in detail for the
actual implementors to cover all aspects.

♦ *Training officer:* If this position exists within
the bank, the person in that position is highly
desirable to serve as a control committee
member. Most projects, whether they be mergers, conversions, software or hardware installations, involve some form of training or
education of staff members. Having the training officer present may provide guidelines and
timeframes as well as actual preparation and
scheduling necessary to the process. Training
is one of the most important tasks in any project plan and, unfortunately, it is most often
underemphasized. A project cannot be successful unless the recipients of the outcome
are educated in its usage. Thus, this function
is vital to the process and a training repre-

sentative should always be a part of the committee.

♦ *Communications officer:* A communications officer is necessary to assess when it is most appropriate to communicate with users and/or external customers on what is occurring with the project in terms of conversion dates and/or implementation. If the project involves the development of new products or services that will be made available to external customers, it will be necessary to begin outlining the requirements for customer notifications—when they will occur and how they will be done. Communications internally or externally, cannot and should not be avoided. Communication officers are professionals who understand when to make communications, to whom, and in what format. Again, much guidance will be provided to the committee by this individual.

♦ *Purchasing officer:* Because all projects involve some form of expenditure, relationship with a vendor, delivery, and so forth, it is prudent to obtain the direction and guidance of the individual who performs purchasing for the bank as his or her primary function. This professional can provide support and assistance in negotiations, obtaining volume purchase agreements, and managing vendor relations. Furthermore, this person will ensure an element of control, through purchase orders, which are sometimes overlooked. In addition, as new equipment is delivered, the purchasing officer can take control of providing storage and other logistical issues that are necessary for uninterrupted handling.

♦ *Operations officer:* The last "control" committee member is that of the operations officer. Because most bank operations officers have much to do with the processing, input, and handling of various transactions, their input can be beneficial. An example of such a contribution involves the need to analyze MICR encoding of documents or changes in the type or size of documents once changes are made. This may be vital to the project but could be overlooked unless the proper representation exists.

It may not be necessary to have all of the "control" committee members involved in each project. Some projects may not involve specific training or compliance issues. However, I have yet to find an instance where a project did not involve these individual disciplines, regardless of the project's type. By involving this type of cadre of expertise, the project manager is building assurance that few issues will be overlooked and that the appropriate advisers are available to raise concerns and issues as early in the project as possible.

Purpose. The overall purpose of the combined committee is to function as a self-contained task force for the completion of the project. The members serve as a sounding board or airing ground for issues, concerns, problems, status, and comments on the project implementation process.

As a necessity, this committee is designed to be a regular forum to bring to the table issues that may be occurring during the process. Without this type of committee, concerns and issues would go unnoticed. This could greatly jeopardize the project process, because lacking a forum, concerns go unresolved or go underground, undermining the overall project.

The committee itself is temporary, in that it exists only throughout the life of the project. On completion of the project, after adequate time for cleanup of loose ends, the committee is disbanded.

Traits/Skills. Committee members are selected on the basis of what they contribute to the overall committee.

Functional committee members must be in a position that will allow them to complete the tasks with existing tools and resources. To accomplish this they must be in control of the functions or areas that will be affected. This would indicate that they would usually be the managers and supervisors in charge of the areas that would be affected by the project. For example, a project that involves the installation and upgrade of teller hardware and/or software must have the teller supervisor or manager as one of the functional committee members. The skills they must bring to the table would be a good understanding of the teller system, how it operates, and ultimately what issues must be considered in any upgrade or transition.

Functional committee members must be individuals who represent and/or manage the departments most affected by the project. It is necessary that they possess a strong operational understanding of their area in order to contribute and actually take part in performing various tasks in the project. In all cases, the project manager must strive to select representatives for this role from each area or department affected by the project.

Furthermore, the functional committee members must have the managerial stature or direct authority to ensure that tasks can be completed within their control. In some cases they will not perform the specific tasks themselves but delegate the tasks to a subordinate or initiate a subcommittee of employees who will actually execute the tasks. In either case, the functional committee member is fully responsible for the timely completion of the tasks, whether performed by him- or herself or through others, and is responsible for reporting this to the project manager and the project committee.

For control committee members, required skills involve a strong understanding of the discipline they represent. Each must be either the manager or representative of the designated area. If a representative, the person must possess not only the knowledge of that function and department but also the ability to think through the issues presented on both a global and conceptual basis. In other words, control committee members must be able to raise issues where pitfalls exist or where more attention is required. They are, in a sense, advisers and are there to provide guidance in their particular area of expertise. In this respect, whoever is selected to participate in these roles must be capable of acting accordingly.

As previously stated, the project committee is the temporary body of employees empowered to implement the project initiated by the organization. This is an absolute must in order to guarantee a successful project implementation, with minimal disruption, within budgeted costs and at the time specified. To that end, project committees cannot be left to chance and are a necessary ingredient in the process. Exhibit 1.3 provides a diagram of the project committee and its functions.

CONCEPTS FOR MANAGING THE PROJECT

As previously referenced in the skills description for the project manager, the primary responsibilities of the project manager are planning, organizing, directing, and controlling all aspects of the project. In order to carry out these responsibilities, project management involves two basic concepts:

♦ Matrix management

♦ Team building

Matrix management, the management of functions and individuals for which no formal reporting relationship exists to achieve a common goal or objective, is an obvious necessity for project management. To move the project in the direction desired, committee members and other subgroups must be managed as

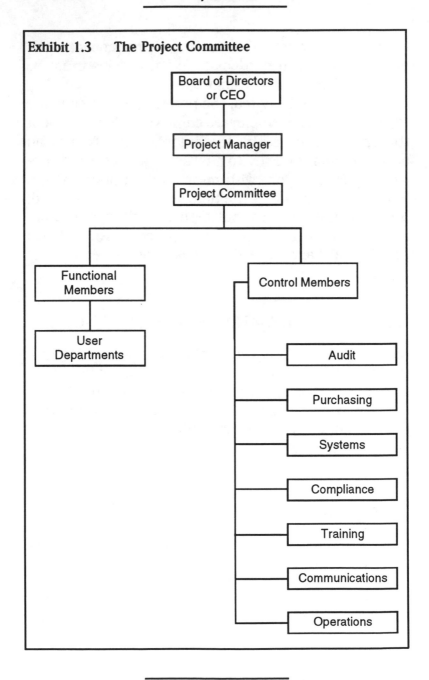

Exhibit 1.3   The Project Committee

Board of Directors or CEO

Project Manager

Project Committee

Functional Members

Control Members

User Departments

Audit

Purchasing

Systems

Compliance

Training

Communications

Operations

if there were a direct reporting relationship. This requires a well-organized manager to establish the controls and monitoring mechanisms necessary to ensure that tasks are carried out correctly in the desired timeframe. This is not necessarily easy, because the traditional managerial leverage tools of appraisals, incentives, salary increases, promotions, and so on, are not available to the project manager. The work performed relies on the shear respect, credibility, and confidence the project manager commands.

As another necessary ingredient, team building is vital. The project itself brings together a number of professionals who would not likely work together in the normal course of business. As a result, a team must be forged from the new group from which to build a sense of purpose, camaraderie, and results. In this type of environment, team building is not easy simply because multiple reporting relationships exist. Both functional and control committee members have regular jobs and are accountable to someone else for them. As a result, there is always some tension about which functions and tasks have priority. The purpose for this discussion is not to discourage project manager candidates but rather to create an awareness of the dynamics that will exist within the committee. For this reason, the project manager selected must be a seasoned manager. Filling this position with a newly hired MBA fresh out of graduate school would make the process difficult and would be an injustice to the candidate. Seasoned managers understand the dynamics of team building and are usually able to command respect and confidence because of their past experiences and successes.

This is one of the most difficult environments in which to manage because of the various complexities, reporting relationships, and volume of tasks. Managing professionals without having legitimate authority requires an ability to garner the confidence and respect of the group without the formal direct reporting relationship typical on the job. Furthermore, because of the temporary nature of the project, the process moves rapidly. There is usually little room for error and/or slack in the schedule. Thus, time management is an absolute prerequisite of all committee members and most certainly in the management process. For this reason, some of the tools discussed in Chapter 2 are the primary aids for ensuring that deadlines are met as prescribed.

SUMMARY

This chapter provided a basic overview of project management for financial institutions. The basic nature of a project was defined, with an understanding of the objectives of project management, which include

♦ Timely completion of planned activities

♦ Implementation of project completion with minimal deviation from time goals

♦ Management of costs to ensure attainment of budgetary projections

♦ Assurance that the objectives and benefits of the project have been attained as originally projected

The need and purpose for effective project management skills in banks was emphasized to minimize any downside risk that would occur without these skills. Because of the changes occurring in banking today, particularly within the realm of technology, financial institutions will continually be implementing new systems, installing and evaluating new hardware and software, and analyzing new concepts for doing business.

The disciplines of project management, for banks, can best be applied in the following areas:

♦ Mergers and conversions

♦ Office automation

♦ Hardware selection and installation

♦ Miscellaneous implementations

♦ Software selection, design, and implementation

It is within these areas that project management skills will provide the greatest payback. The purpose for this book is not only to provide the fundamental skills of project management but also to provide actual examples, based on experience, for specific applications that financial institutions are likely to encounter.

The benefits of project management are many, the primary considerations of which fall within these: reduced costs, reduced opportunity for error, greater control and knowledge of product status, and management development as a by-product.

The nature and understanding of projects were also discussed focusing on two basic project types: terminal and developmental projects. Terminal projects tend to be ones that are clearly defined, with a beginning and end. When this type of project ends there is no continuation or residue. Developmental projects, on the other hand, may be characterized as starter or initiation projects that lead into larger projects. Projects have an impact on the organization as a whole, depending on their size. It is important to understand the global nature of projects and recognize the fact that they are likely to change or impact the day-to-day world of a number of employees. Change is difficult, and project managers and committee members alike must be sensitive to these effects on the organization as they proceed.

Projects begin or are originated based on criteria that identify whether the formal application of the project management discipline should be initiated. Following are the criteria for this determination:

♦ Three or more individuals will be involved in implementing the tasks.

♦ Several tasks must be completed.

♦ The tasks must be completed over a period of time (at least one month).

♦ The tasks may be interdependent.

♦ Tasks must be performed at specified times in order to be successful.

Applying these basic rules will provide assistance in determining when and when not to initiate project status.

No discussion of project management is complete without a good understanding of the support and commitment required to be successful. This is not only handy to have but imperative for the type of change and assimilation that will be taking place as a result of the project. Because of the matrix management structure of projects and the pervasive impact the structure has on the organization, management must endorse and embrace the project establishing the commitment and tone for the organization.

The project process is typically organized and structured in two primary components: the project manager and the project committee. Project managers must possess strong managerial skills, particularly emphasizing the ability to manage a number of professionals and users in a matrix management mode. Other important aspects of the project manager consist of the specific skills and their associated traits, reporting relationships, roles and function, and (ultimately) how this individual is selected. An actual job description is provided as well to aid in the understanding of this individual's duties. The project committee is generally composed of both functional and control members. Functional committee members are, for the most part, the managers or users of the systems or project to be implemented. Their role is to actually perform the tasks themselves or through subcommittees during the project process. Control committee members, on the other hand, serve more in an advisory capacity, representing staff functions in the organizations that can provide input to the process necessary for successful completion. These control areas are:

♦ Audit

♦ Systems and programming

♦ Compliance

♦ Training

♦ Communications

♦ Purchasing

♦ Operations

The roles/responsibilities, traits and skills, and purpose of these committee members were further defined in the chapter.

The scope of the project is important to define formally. The scope statement provides the boundaries within which the project will operate. Project scopes tend to eliminate guesswork and serve to eliminate potentially disruptive interpretations.

Finally, the act of managing the project itself was discussed. Emphasis is placed on two elements for successful project management: matrix management and team building. The art of managing the project cannot be taken lightly; once the process begins, it demands strict ongoing attention. Because the project team members themselves typically have other jobs with no formal reporting relationship to the project manager, team-building skills are an absolute must. This requires the ability to motivate and be able to effectively delegate and work through others in a matrix environment.

NOTES

1. James P. Lewis, *The Project Manager's Desk Reference* (Chicago: Probus Publishing, 1993).

2. *Webster's II New Riverside Dictionary,* (New York: Barclay Books, 1984).

3. James A. Stoner, *Management* (Englewood Cliffs, N.J.: Prentice Hall, 1978).

2

Project Management Tools

As with any profession, it is difficult to be successful without the proper tools to do the job. For project managers, the necessary tools are essentially information and feedback-type mechanisms. Feedback alone is a primary ingredient of the tools used by project managers. Similar to the use of a bathroom scale, during a weight loss program, the scale becomes a tool that measures the progress made with a project.

Because project management places a heavy emphasis on time, most of the tools are structured around timeframes. The purpose of this chapter is to explain the primary tools used in the project management process.

This book's emphasis is project management for banks, so the tools and charts used are geared toward nontechnical professionals. Much care has been taken to use and illustrate tools that can be shown and explained to a diverse group of individuals without the fear of becoming "too technical" and losing the audience. The tools explained in this chapter have actually been used and well tested for usage with bank staff members, from tellers to CEOs. Such empirical evidence of their benefits is important, because one of the goals of project management is meeting and communicating timeframes and progress. This can only be accomplished with mechanisms that can readily be understood by a broad audience.

Many of the tools can be obtained in the marketplace packaged in various types of software. In the author's experience, many of these become too technical or too busy and don't lend themselves well to widespread distribution. This is not to say they are bad; they are generally very good packages. For banks, however, there is seldom a great need to track milestones, slack time, or even the critical path in some cases. This is not true when it comes to building submarines, skyscrapers, software, or a new model of computer. The point is that most financial institutions are not likely to immerse themselves with those types of highly technical issues. Generally, banks use consultants or contract out for such services.

The emphasis of this book is project management skills for bankers for projects to be conducted by bankers and the means to plan for greater success in completing the projects that financial institutions perform internally. Because the types of projects and applications for these approaches will directly affect bank users, the project's success rests on having mechanisms that can be used and understood by bank users.

The primary tools used for financial institutions' projects are discussed in this chapter. The outline will be limited to the following:

♦ Project plan

♦ Gantt chart (timeline)

♦ Time matrix

♦ Critical path method network

♦ Calendar and tickler

♦ Project template

For each tool, the purpose, how it is used, and examples are provided. The intent is to provide readers with actual examples that can be emulated in the process of the reader's own projects.

In all cases, the examples illustrated require no sophisticated software package, with the possible exception of the CPM network model. Everything else has been developed using Lotus 1-2-3© and a WYSI-WYG (What You See Is What You Get) reportmaker package.

PROJECT PLAN

The project plan is the primary tool used for any project that is undertaken. The purpose of the project plan is to provide the foundation and framework for the project. It literally is the blueprint for what must be accomplished in the project. Project plans can be quite lengthy, because they contain every task that will be performed throughout the project. Following are the main elements of a standard project plan:

♦ Project tasks and activities

♦ Responsible person

♦ Weeks required

♦ Beginning date

♦ Target completion date

♦ Actual completion date

♦ Status

♦ *Project tasks and activities:* All physical actions or activities that must take place during the life of the project. These functions can be segmented or bundled under major headings or events.

♦ *Responsible person:* This category is available to record the name of the professional who is responsible for completing the tasks indicated.

♦ *Weeks precutover required:* This number is for planning purposes and indicates the number of weeks (or specified time interval) that the task must be started in advance of the implementation date of the project (cutover date).

♦ *Beginning date:* This represents the date on which the task is projected to start.

♦ *Target completion date:* This date, proposed at the onset of the project plan, is the one on which the task is estimated to be completed.

♦ *Actual completion date:* This is the date on which the task is actually completed.

♦ *Status:* This section reports task progress, problems, issues, or concerns during the course of the project life.

A sample standard project plan is illustrated in Exhibit 2.1.

Project plans provide organization to the project as well as a means of planning the project. It literally becomes the underlying document which records the detail of every aspect of the project which is to occur, much like the assembly instructions of a piece of equipment. A project cannot be properly conducted without a project plan.

Development and Usage

In order for the project to get off to a good start, it must begin with the development of the project plan. The development and maintenance of this plan is the responsibility of the project manager. This effort begins by creating an outline of all tasks and activities that will occur during the scope of the project. The project plan sheet, as illustrated in Exhibit 2.1, is used to record the tasks and activities in the designated area of the plan. As previously stated, this record can be

Exhibit 2.1   Sample Blank Standard Project Plan

Event/Activity	Responsible	Weeks Precutover	Target Begin	Target End	Actual End	Status

relativiely large and will likely require more than one page.

Activities, Events, and Milestones. Project plans generally do not emphasize the relationship of activities to one another but rather ensure that all activities are recorded and accounted for. When developing the outline of activities to be performed, the project manager and team must consider the scope of the project to know the boundaries within which to define what must be accomplished. The development of this portion of the project plan will involve the identification of activities, events, and milestones.

- ♦ *Activities*: Activities relate to the physical work or action that must be taken to complete the desired outcome.

- ♦ *Events:* Events are categories of activities that summarize the result of the activities into a final planned outcome.

- ♦ *Milestone:* A milestone is an event of very significant importance to the project. It is designated or highlighted as a point of achievement or plateau that has been attained. It earmarks a point of evaluation of project performance at a point in time.

The project manager begins to develop this section of the project plan by separately listing major events that must occur to complete the project. Once this is accomplished, a specific set of activities associated with each event can then be developed. This activities list assumes a classic outline form as the following example illustrates:

I. Installation of an end-user computing system in the bank.
    A. Complete the hardware request for proposal (RFP)

    1.   Identify and develop a list of potential vendors.

    2.   Develop a list of needs which must be addressed by each vendor for consideration.

    3.   Prepare the RFP, incorporating the needs which must be addressed.

    4.   Mail the RFPs to the selected vendors.

The initial heading (Roman numeral one) is the project heading itself. This would typically be displayed at the top of the project plan as shown in Exhibit 2.1. The major heading (letter A) of, "The completion of the hardware request for proposal (RFP)" is a major event. This also could be a milestone for the project, although it is not necessarily. Because the project plan is the blueprint for the completion of the project, the specific activities required must be identified and recorded. As in the example, the four activities shown are the steps necessary for the completion of the request for proposal. The reason this is done is to ensure that nothing is missed and that it is clear what must be accomplished in order to achieve the ultimate event.

The project manager may not be the only person to identify all of the activities to be accomplished. This should be a collaborative effort encompassing members of the project committee as well as any vendors or consultants involved in the process. The project plan should be completed as soon as the project is endorsed and the scope of the project is defined. This helps to ensure that all activities and events are identified early before the project formally begins. Once the project is in process, it is difficult to go back and identify activities in the midst of implementation.

The activities developed may also be identified through flow charting. Chapter 5 provides actual activities and events for specific bank projects that may prove helpful.

Assigning Responsibility. Once all of the events and activities are identified and recorded on the preliminary project plan, the next step is to identify who will complete the tasks. Responsibility should be assigned to each activity recorded in the preliminary project plan. Although events and milestones are not activities, overall responsibility can be assigned for an event. The responsible party usually is a member of the project committee. This does not indicate that he or she will complete each activity but rather is responsible for all activities associated with the event, which the committee member can choose to delegate.

Assignment of responsibility can occur at the initial kickoff meeting of the project committee or prior to that. In either case, however, care must be taken to ensure that the individual who is assigned to the task is either part of the project committee or a designated participant in a subcommittee group. Not only must the staff member be aware of what is assigned to him or her, it must be ascertained whether the committee member has the time and the necessary approval to complete the task. Again, this is where matrix management is useful. Ideally, the most likely or most knowledgeable person is the one assigned responsibility for the activity. In addition, it is highly desirable for that person to have input in the process, because this will only help to solidify the sense of responsibility and ownership necessary for completion.

As a final note, the assignment of responsibility should never be taken lightly. These are, after all, the people who will make or break the project. For this reason, individuals should be selected who have a strong sense of urgency, are responsible, and are characterized as "doers" in the organization. In many cases the people assigned are already committee members. In other cases, the committee members may delegate certain activities. In the case of delegated tasks, one of the committee members must take responsibility for ensuring that the assignment is actually carried out. In project management, where timing is everything, taking the time to ensure that a workable network exists, for execution, can only improve the process.

Assigning Dates. Three dates will ultimately be established, two of which must be determined at the onset of the project:

♦ Beginning date

♦ Target completion date

Both dates are targets or planned events. They must be planned in advance and recorded in order to manage the entire process. The third date is not a planned event but the *actual completion date*. This date is assigned and recorded only upon completion of the tasks. The actual completion date is used to compare the planned timing to the actual, thus enabling not only closure but also a measure of performance in terms of slippage. *Slippage* is a project management term that indicates the amount of time the actual completion date exceeded the planned target date. For example, if an activity was to be completed on June 20 but was actually completed on June 30, 10 days of slippage occurred. This may not be detrimental to the project unless the task is on the critical path for other activities. The critical path will be described later in the chapter.

Beginning and targeted completion dates should be assigned by the individual assigned to complete the activity and in conjunction with the project manager. To assign these dates, some advance preparation is necessary. Planned activities must be targeted based upon the overall timeframe of the project. To assign such dates, these steps should be followed:

1.   Determine the overall project timeframe planned. This is the overall window of time that is estimated to complete the project. The range of dates should be expressed in num-

ber of weeks or months rather than actual calendar dates. An example of this could be 6 months, 20 weeks, or 18 months.

The window of time should extend for the entire project, allowing for wrap-up or review time after implementation. In general, the implementation or cutover is not the end of the project. Cutover dates are typically week zero. Any clean-up or wrap-up for follow-up will be in negative numbers.

2. Review the preliminary project plan and rank order the major events, not activities, in order of implementation. That is, array them in the order of anticipated completion that makes sense. For example, the development of a concept design must occur before the selection of a software vendor, and this would occur before formal training. Not all major events will logically fall into a sequential order; some have equal weight in terms of when they should be completed. These events can occur concurrently with other events.

3. Begin at the end of the project timeline (week zero) or the approximate end of the project. Select the last major event in the rank ordering of events and determine how many weeks in advance of the cutover or implementation date it should be completed. As an example, "training" could be a major event. Because training occurs at the end of the timeline, it should be determined when training must

occur or be completed in advance of the cutover date. This process should be applied to
each major event, beginning with the last
event in the list moving in reverse order.

4. Once all events have been assigned a time
    (number of weeks) in advance of the imple-
    mentation, the timeframes should be re-
    corded on the project plan in the section
    labeled "weeks precutover." An example of
    this is shown in Exhibit 2.2.

5. The next step is to determine the time interval
    for completion of each activity associated
    with the event prior to actual implementa-
    tion. If this event indicates it must be com-
    pleted by week 10, as shown in Exhibit 2.2,
    this means that all activities associated with
    this event must be completed prior to this.
    For each activity, then, a completion time
    interval should be determined. Again, as
    shown in Exhibit 2.2, the first activity, "de-
    termine vendors" should be completed by in-
    terval fourteen (or week fourteen) in advance
    of implementation (week zero). The remaining
    activities can then be determined in similar
    format. It is important to note that no activity
    should have an interval less than that of the
    event. In all cases the intervals should equal
    or exceed that of the events.

When establishing time intervals the project manager should determine these with the appropriate

Exhibit 2.2 Assigning People and Timeframes to Events on the Project Plan

Event/Activity	Responsible	Weeks Precutover	Target Begin	Target End	Actual End	Status
A. COMPLETE THE REQUEST FOR PROPOSAL	J. Smith	10				
1. Determine vendors	R. Jones	14				
2. Develop needs list	T. Jenkins	12				
3. Prepare RFP	J. Smith	11				
4. Mail RFP	P. Roberts	10				

party responsible for the event and activities. The final step is to establish the beginning and targeted completion dates. This assignment is not a time interval but an actual calendar date. In order to assign these dates begin with the targeted completion using the following steps:

1. Using the overall timeframe for the project duration, the project manager should identify the calendar date of the implementation or cutover. Generally, this is expressed in terms of the week, beginning with the date or month. For example, if a cutover is to occur during the middle of the week, the actual implementation time would be expressed as the date of the beginning of the week (Monday).

2. Once the actual week of cutover is established, this date becomes week zero. For each activity, then, an actual date can be established for its completion. The best way to explain this is by the following example:

    ♦ If the cutover date is established as June 30, 199X, this occurs in midweek. Therefore, the cutover week would be June 28, which is the beginning of the week (Monday). This becomes week "zero." Using the example in Exhibit 2.2 we count backwards from week zero to establish completion dates for each activity. Beginning with the activity closest to week "zero" the following is determined:

Week #	Event/Activity	Actual Week of
0	Cutover	6/28/9X
1		6/21/9X
2		6/14/9X
3		6/07/9X
4		5/31/9X
5		5/24/9X
6		5/17/9X
7		5/10/9X
8		5/03/9X
9		4/26/9X
10	Mail RFP	4/19/9X
11	Prepare RFP	4/12/9X
12	Develop needs list	4/05/9X
13		3/29/9X
14	Determine vendors	3/22/9X

3. In the previous example, the targeted completion date has now been determined and can be recorded on the project plan. This is illustrated in Exhibit 2.3.

With the establishment of targeted completion dates, the beginning dates for the activities can be determined. Unlike the target dates, beginning dates are set by the amount of time necessary to complete the activity. The time required for each activity is determined by the committee member responsible for the activity, in conjunction with the project manager.

Exhibit 2.3   Adding Targeted Completion Dates to Events on the Project Plan

Event/Activity	Responsible	Weeks Precutover	Target Begin	Target End	Actual End	Status
A. COMPLETE THE REQUEST FOR PROPOSAL	J. Smith	10				
1. Determine vendors	R. Jones	14		3/22/93		
2. Develop needs list	T. Jenkins	12		4/05/93		
3. Prepare RFP	J. Smith	11		4/12/93		
4. Mail RFP	P. Roberts	10		4/19/93		

The individual who will be performing the activity will know best how much time is required to complete it. In order to do this, the management team uses the following steps:

1. Begin with the first activity or the activity farthest from the implementation or cutover date.

2. Determine, from the individual responsible for the task, how much time should be allotted for its completion. The time allotted should be expressed in terms of a time interval rather than actual time in terms of hours and minutes. For example, the activity for determining who the vendors will be may be accomplished within two weeks. Although the actual process may require less actual time, the person responsible is committing to having this task completed within a two-week timeframe. Such "padding" of the schedule is perfectly acceptable, because the committee members responsible for the activities must take into account their other, nonproject-related duties for which they are also accountable.

3. Once the time interval is established, the actual beginning date is determined by counting backward from the targeted completion (calendar) date. Using the example in Exhibit 2.2, if the time interval for the first

activity is set at two weeks, the actual beginning date would be March 8, 199X.

4. This backward time-setting is repeated for each activity, recording all beginning dates on the project plan as illustrated in Exhibit 2.4.

The role of the project manager in this process is evaluating each time-completion commitment made and reviewing it against the overall project implementation window. If the time interval is unreasonably long, the project manager has to negotiate a more reasonable timespan. This may necessitate adding additional resources to the activity or seeking to relieve some of the day-to-day responsibilities of the committee member to allow him or her more time to devote to the tasks at hand. Without this type of involvement the project window would not be met and would exceed the time desired by management for installation or implementation. In some cases this slippage may not be of concern, but in others, implementation deadlines may be mandated by regulations or other directives that stipulate that the dates cannot be changed. In this circumstance, negotiating for more resources or fewer outside responsibilities will ensure that all tasks are completed within the time allotted.

Now that each activity has both a beginning and targeted completion date established, it is possible to set the timeline of the event. Recall that the event is the overall category that was originally prioritized. In Exhibit 2.4, the event, "Complete the request for pro-

Exhibit 2.4   Adding Targeted Begin Dates to Events on the Project Plan

Event/Activity	Responsible	Weeks Precutover	Target Begin	Target End	Actual End	Status
A. COMPLETE THE REQUEST FOR PROPOSAL	J. Smith	10				
1. Determine vendors	R. Jones	14	3/08/93	3/22/93		
2. Develop needs list	T. Jenkins	12	3/22/93	4/05/93		
3. Prepare RFP	J. Smith	11	4/05/93	4/12/93		
4. Mail RFP	P. Roberts	10	4/12/93	4/19/93		

posal" can now have a timeline. This is accomplished by recording the beginning date of the activity within the event that is begun first—in this case, "Determine vendors." This is the earliest start date of March 8, 199X. The end date for the event is taken from the targeted completion date of the activity with the latest targeted completion date. In Exhibit 2.4, this is April 19, 199X for the activity, "Mail RFP." Once this process is complete, the entire event will have a timeline of March 8, 199X through April 19, 199X to complete the request for proposal, a period of six weeks. These dates are recorded on the project plan, as shown in Exhibit 2.5.

Finally, the actual completion date is left blank until the activity is actually completed. Completion dates will occur, and should be updated, periodically throughout the life of the project. The status section, as well, is left blank until issues arise with respect to the event or activities. Although usage of the project plan will be discussed more fully in the next chapter, its "status" section is used as a means of communicating ongoing needs or issues that may jeopardize dates, or that are important to the process. Once the activity is completed, the word *complete* is recorded in this column.

GANTT CHART

Definition and Purpose

The Gantt chart is another key project management tool. It receives its name from Henry L. Gantt, a contemporary of such scientific management pioneers as

Exhibit 2.5   Adding Targeted Begin and End Dates for an Entire Event

Event/Activity	Responsible	Weeks Precutover	Target Begin	Target End	Actual End	Status
A. COMPLETE THE REQUEST FOR PROPOSAL	J. Smith	10	3/08/93	4/19/93		
1. Determine vendors	R. Jones	14	3/08/93	3/22/93		
2. Develop needs list	T. Jenkins	12	3/22/93	4/05/93		
3. Prepare RFP	J. Smith	11	4/05/93	4/12/93		
4. Mail RFP	P. Roberts	10	4/12/93	4/19/93		

Frederick Taylor, Frank and Lillian Gilbreth, and Henry Fayol. Gantt actually participated in the landmark Midvale steel experiments that launched the field of scientific management and Frederick Taylor as its founding father. Gantt developed the chart, which carries his name, as a management tool used to show and track the actual timeline within which project events and activities must take place.

Gantt charts enable the project manager, project committee members, and senior management to see the entire project, and its key elements, in terms of the overall time constraints under which the project is being run. The importance of this tool is second only to that of the project plan and should be used in conjunction with the project plan (as will be explained later in this section).

Gantt charts consist of two primary elements:

♦ *Project events and/or activities:* These items are the actual description of the event or activity to occur. They are, essentially, the same items found in the project plan.

♦ *Calendar dates:* Calendar dates are arrayed from left to right in chronological sequence dependent on the time interval selected. This can be days, weeks, months, quarters, or even years.

Exhibit 2.6 illustrates a standard Gantt chart.

Beyond the two elements of project events and calendar dates, the distinguishing feature of the Gantt chart is the visual display of the beginning and ending

Exhibit 2.6   Beginning a Gantt Chart

Events	JAN 4 11 18 25	FEB 1 8 15 22	MAR 1 8 15 22 29	APR 5 12 19 26	MAY 3 10 17 24 31	JUN 7 14 21 28	JUL 5 12 19 26	AUG 2 9 16 23 30	SEP 6 13 20 27	OCT 4 11 18 25	NOV 1 8 15 22	DEC 6 13 20 27
1. Complete the request for proposal			▭									

timeframes for the completion of the events or activities. A line connecting the beginning and ending dates is known as a timeline. This graphically shows the project management group the time allocated to the specific activity for the purposes of both planning and monitoring the project. It provides a quick, easy way to determine what must happen, and when, in the life of the entire project. Exhibit 2.6 shows a single timeline taken from the project plan.

Development and Usage

The previous section described the steps involved in developing the project plan in its entirety. As emphasized, the project plan should seldom be given short shrift. It outlines every step, in the form of activities and events, that must occur. Without this prerequisite, the Gantt chart cannot be completed, because the source of the information for this Gantt chart is the project plan.

The Gantt chart, like the project plan, is the responsibility of the project manager. The project manager updates this document regularly to chart project progress and communicates the status to appropriate parties.

For the purposes of this book, the approach is to develop simplified Gantt charts that are readily readable by all pertinent parties. Many software products on the market produce Gantt charts easily. However, before the project team purchases a package, they should ensure that the charts generated will be readable by a nontechnical audience, such as bank staff and management. The primary purpose of this book is to outline a project management process for bankers, not for rocket scientists or engineers. In managing a number of projects for banks, I have found that the more detailed the timeline, the more difficult it is to read. Most senior executives and individuals who are a party to this process are bankers by profession. As such, if they are to be successful in completing all of the activities required, with a degree of precision, project plans and Gantt charts must be as simplified as possible.

Because of this, the Gantt charts illustrated are relatively simple, and are not generally cluttered with a number of symbols and other indicators which tend to confuse readers. The charts illustrated can be developed without purchasing technical software and could be developed by hand, if desired. Generally, the charts shown are developed using Lotus 1-2-3© and WYSIWYG (What You See Is What You Get) for reporting development and printing.

Before the chart creation is explained, there are a few terms which are important to understand, because they are used in the development and monitoring of the charts. These items are literally the outcome of a review of a Gantt chart. They provide the status on the events and activities in terms of

♦ Planned timelines

♦ Completed timelines

♦ Slack time

♦ Slippage

Once the Gantt chart is developed and subsequently updated by the project manager, these four items will become readily evident.

♦ *Planned timelines:* When the Gantt chart is developed, the first item formally displayed is the "planned" timeline for each event or activity. This is simply the timeline (beginning and ending dates connected) indicated from the project plan. Usually this is expressed in the form of a line, bar, or some other form of line (X's). The easiest to read is a bar as shown in Exhibit 2.6.

♦ *Completed timeline:* Completed timelines are illustrated by shaded or darkened lines differentiating them from a "planned" or "in process" timeline. When the project is complete, all lines will be shaded or darkened.

♦ *Slack time:* Slack time is a technical term used to indicate the presence of "additional" time beyond that planned for the event or activity to begin. Every activity or event has a targeted beginning date for project management purposes. However, if some activities do not begin as planned but start later, although the delay does not cause the project deadlines to slip as a whole, slack time exists. If activity timelines overlap (occur concurrently), slack time also exists. If one activity depends solely on another, no slack time exists, because any delay in the start of the first activity will delay the start of the next activity and may impact the project as a whole.[1] Slack time will be explored more fully later in this section.

♦ *Slippage:* Slippage is a term used to indicate how much the planned event or activity timeline has been delayed or extended, for a variety of reasons. Slippage is illustrated in the timeline by extending the line to the new target, but differentiating it in some way from the planned timeline. If bars are used, the new target could be a light shading or diagonal lines indicating the additional time added to the timeline.

Now that some of the key terms used for management tools have been defined, the remaining parts of this section provide the steps necessary to develop and use the Gantt chart.

Events and Activities

Unlike project plans, Gantt charts are limited in length; that is, they are summarized based on key information contained in the project plan. Recall from the project plan development section that the first step in developing the plan is identifying the primary "events" or categories of activities that will occur throughout the life of the project. From these events, detailed activities are determined. Because the Gantt chart is a management tool that charts progress, only the primary events or categories are recorded in this section. In other words, it is not necessary to record every activity, because this is already recorded in the project plan; only the major events should be recorded.

The reason for this is that the purpose of the Gantt chart is to show the entire project in a capsulated form. It provides a "snapshot" of where the project and events are at a point in time.

Using the project plan as the source of information for the Gantt chart, the project management team records only the "events" in this section of the chart. In an earlier example (Exhibit 2.5), "Complete the request for proposal" is an event, because it indicates a specific point in time when the action is performed. In this case, that point is an ending point. It is not necessary to record the individual activities, because these will be incorporated in the overall timeline for the event. All other events would then be recorded in the Gantt chart for the entire project, as shown in Exhibit 2.7.

Activities can also be recorded in this section of the Gantt chart. In some cases, a project manager may wish to highlight or record a specific important activity for tracking. This practice is certainly acceptable. The only caution is to avoid recording each and every activity on the Gantt chart. This will detract from its usefulness as a "snapshot" scheduling and tracking report. Especially in large projects, the volume of activities are best left to the project plan; otherwise, the Gantt chart becomes too cumbersome to use as a tool.

Exhibit 2.7   Adding Events to the Gantt Chart

Events											
1. Process kickoff											
2. Complete the concept design											
3. Complete the request for proposal											
4. Software selection											
5. Testing											
6. Training											
7. Installation											

Calendar Dates

The next part of the Gantt chart is the section indicating the time intervals and actual calendar dates for completion of the events. In this section, each column heading is assigned a date. Each subsequent column is dated in accordance with the specific time interval. For instance, if the time interval selected is weekly, each column indicates the date on which the week begins in chronological order to the end of the chart. The intervals used can be days, weeks, months, quarters, or years, depending on the overall life (duration) of the project. When developing this section of the Gantt chart, the project manager should first determine the project time window. If this is one year, six months, or some other time duration, he or she should endeavor to reflect the entire time on the Gantt chart, from start to finish.

The next step is to determine the time interval that fits most appropriately for managing the project. In most cases, weekly intervals are best; however, if the project duration is long (four to five years) quarterly intervals may be used to reflect the entire project life on one page. The first column reflects the calendar time in which the project actually begins. In the example previously used, the event, "Complete the request for proposal," occurs within the timeframe of March and April of 199X. Therefore, the dates reflected in the time interval section of the chart must reflect these dates at least. However, the project itself begins prior to this time and ends later than the completion of the activities for that event. The Gantt chart should reflect the project duration, from beginning to end.

Exhibit 2.8   Entering the Project's Starting and Ending Dates

Events	JAN 4 11 18 25	FEB 1 8 15 22	MAR 1 8 15 22 29	APR 5 12 19 26	MAY 3 10 17 24 31	JUN 7 14 21 28	JUL 5 12 19 26	AUG 2 9 16 23 30	SEP 6 13 20 27	OCT 4 11 18 25	NOV 1 8 15 22	DEC 6 13 20 27
1. Process kickoff												
2. Complete the concept design												
3. Complete the request for proposal												
4. Software selection												
5. Testing												
6. Training												
7. Installation												

The starting and ending dates can be determined from the project plan. An example of a project plan with completed time intervals is shown in Exhibit 2.8.

Timelines

The last part of the Gantt chart is the actual timeline. The timeline is the graphical portion of the Gantt chart that illustrates, visually, the time span for each event or activity recorded (calendar beginning and ending dates). This is the most important section of the chart, because it provides a snapshot of the project progress, event overlap, and various other aspects of the project at a glance. These charted activities make Gantt charts tremendous project management tools, because they can be used for planning, illustrating progress, or simply comparing activities for contention.

Because Gantt charts are an effective means of showing progress "at a glance," they can be shared with a broad audience, from CEOs on down. For this reason, however, it is important that the charts remain simple to read.

Many of the project management software products today are good; however, they become overly technical and laden with symbols. Although this display is descriptive for engineers, it is not conducive for presentation to senior bank executives and other nontechnical users. Because Gantt charts are tools for project communication and progress, it behooves the project manager to keep them as simple as possible. Because of the need for straightforward presentation, only three stages of the timelines are used in this process:

♦ Planned timeline

♦ Extensions or slippage

♦ Completed events

Each of these stages is shown graphically using horizontal bars, as in a bar chart. The exhibits shown previously are all completed using Lotus 1-2-3© v. 2.3, with the WYSIWYG (What You See Is What You Get) feature, which allows more professional chart development. Using this software enables the project manager to shade the bars to indicate progress. Although Lotus 1-2-3© (with WYSIWYG) is helpful, these charts can also be developed manually on a posterboard, greaseboard, or blackboard for presentation purposes.

The following types of bars have proven to be descriptive and easy to read for the three primary stages:

Stage	In Lotus 1-2-3	Manual
1. Planned timeline		
2. Extension or slippage		
3. Completed event		

Planned Timeline. The planned timeline is simply a clear (noncolored or shaded) bar that extends from the beginning time interval until the time it is targeted to be completed. Exhibit 2.9 shows this type of bar for some of the events scheduled. The planned

Exhibit 2.9   Adding Shaded Bars to Denote Slippage

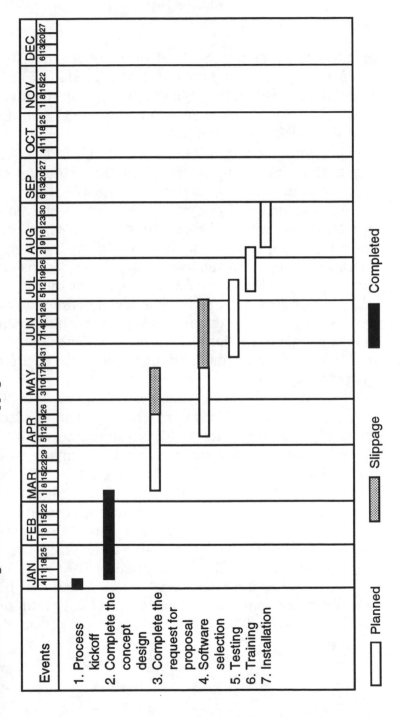

timeline, once set and recorded, does not change. This is done to evaluate the validity and precision of time estimates as well as the ability of the project manager to ensure their timely completion. The only time the planned timeline bars should be altered is if an extension is required or slippage has occurred. In this case, the original bar is unchanged, but the extension or slippage is added to it, as explained next.

Extension or Slippage. Some activities or events inevitably are delayed for various reasons. When this occurs, the slippage must be reflected on the Gantt chart as a new targeted completion date. To reflect these changes, the original clear bar is left intact. An addition is reflected by shading a new timeline leading from the end of the original planned completion to the new targeted completion. In this way, senior managers and users can see that a change has occurred from the original plans.

This reflection of targeted versus actual dates is important; if the timelines were simply recast to reflect the change, the revisions could continually occur without showing the consequences of the slippage, and eventually they would jeopardize the entire project. Management would be misled and would ultimately be affected by delays that they would not be aware of. By reflecting the changes on the Gantt chart, management and project members alike will be well aware of the slippage and will seek to make up the lost time. In other words, the visual cue of the added, darker bars provides some motivation to accelerate and get back on schedule. Noting one slippage point visually also helps the project team discern the impact the extension will have on other targeted dates.

The slippage may also affect when the event was targeted to start. In this case, the same shaded bars should be added, except to the left end of the clear bars, to reflect the new start within the planned timeline.

All extensions can be reflected by shading the new timeline (beginning to end) or drawing an extended bar and putting diagonal lines in it. Exhibit 2.9 illustrates how the Gantt chart looks when slippage times are included.

Completed Event. The final stage is the actual completed event. A completed event is one in which all activities associated with the event have been accomplished. Only then is the entire event complete. This date is determined from the project plan, because it is the document used on a day-to-day basis to record such items as complete.

The event timeline, then, must be reflected as completed by darkening the bar (solid black) the entire length of the planned bar. This solid line indicates that the event is fully completed. Again, Exhibit 2.9 gives examples of such bars for completed activities.

Thus, the reader of the Gantt chart can ascertain, at a glance, where the project currently is at a given point in time. To add further readability to the chart, a descriptive heading is necessary. The heading denotes the name of the project. Immediately beneath it is the date of the chart. This represents the last date on which the chart was updated and is therefore reflected as an "as of" date. Similar to a balance sheet financial statement, the "as of" date reflects the period ending on which the chart is prepared. Finally, a legend, recorded at the bottom of the Gantt chart, provides explanations for the types of bars shown on the chart. This provides definition for the casual reader so that anyone reading the chart can understand it immediately.

The Gantt chart, as previously stated, is best used as a management and project update vehicle. Its frequency of update depends on how often the project committee meets or how frequently status reports are to be delivered to senior management. Virtually every time the project committee meets the Gantt chart should be brought up to date. This is done by first updating the project plan from which event and activity status is determined. From this information, the Gantt chart is reviewed and changed to reflect the current status. Actual changes are made to the timelines based on project results that are discussed at the project committee meetings.

Updated Gantt charts should be delivered to senior management and/or to the sponsors of the project at regular intervals to communicate project status. Regular updates are monthly, at a minimum, or more frequent depending on the needs of the sponsor. However, it is infeasible to require updates more frequently than every other week—at least until the final stages of the project, when deadlines tend to tighten. To do so would not likely produce any tangible information from which to become more informed.

Because of the audience viewing these reports, the basic Gantt chart illustrated is easy to understand

and can be shown to a wide variety of readers. It is an effective means of communicating project status without becoming "too technical" and should be used in conjunction, as a primary project management tool, with the project plan.

TIME MATRIX

Definition and Purpose

Time matrices are supplemental project management tools that can be used for limited purposes. In general, the time matrix is a sort of planner that is used to schedule key events or milestones for the project. Time matrices are not used solely for specific projects but also to schedule key events in order to evaluate overlap and/or conflict with other events. This document is most useful for project managers in organizations that have a variety of events occurring within a relatively narrow window of time.

Time matrices are similar to Gantt charts in that they reflect a snapshot of what will occur within a broad time period. They differ from Gantt charts in the way information is reflected. Rather than show the period of time in which a specific event will be completed or carried out (from beginning to end) it reflects a specific major event or milestone by the day or week of completion. In this way, the major event can be scheduled or planned in conjunction with other events to avoid time conflicts and overlap.

The primary elements of the time matrix are similar to the Gantt chart, as follows:

♦ *Major events:* These items represent a major occurrence in a particular project. This is not necessarily the "event" as indicated in the project plan or Gantt chart but rather the primary milestone that occurs in the project.

♦ *Calendar week:* The calendar week is the actual date of the beginning of each week, starting with Monday. These are recorded on the left-hand side of this report. Although usually the left column reflects weeks, it can also list days for short, intensive projects.

An example of a time matrix is shown in Exhibit 2.10.

Using the two elements, the primary feature of the time matrix is the ability to record what major events are occurring at a specific time. In this way, the matrix can be used to schedule major events to avoid conflicts or down time.

Development

The time matrix is not a mandatory project management tool but a supplementary chart used for a number of purposes. The matrix is used in conjunction with the project plan, in particular, and as a source for the information contained in the time matrix.

As with all project management tools, the time matrix is developed and used directly by the project manager. Its development relies on the data contained in the individual project plans. As previously reflected, the time matrix is effective as a planning and infor-

Exhibit 2.10   A Time Matrix Template

Week of	Telephone Training	Microcomputer Project Kickoff	Cabling Completed	Microcomputer Training	Telephone Cutover	Microcomputer Installation
1-4-93						
1-11-93						
1-18-93						
1-25-93						
2-1-93						
2-8-93						
2-15-93						
2-22-15						
3-1-93						
3-8-93						
3-15-93						
3-22-93						
3-29-93						

mational tool to assess the occurrence of major events. It is beneficial when a number of projects are occurring either simultaneously or within a short span of time of one another. However, it can also be used to plan when major events or milestones of a single project are to occur. The reason this is important is that when originally establishing milestones or major events, it is possible that some tasks may overlap with others using the same staff or resources, or the tasks may be scheduled too closely together. Particularly as it relates to events such as training and actual cutovers, where many people are involved, this type of planner is most beneficial.

Major Events. The project manager develops the matrix in conjunction with the project plan. Recall from the project plan section of this chapter that the development of a list of events is one of the first stages of development. From this initial list of events, there are key events or milestones that should be highlighted from the list. These items in turn compose the column heads atop the time matrix. In most cases, major events or milestones consist of the occurrence of a major part of the project that typically represents a major change or impacts the users or employees of the bank. Examples of major events or milestones in a typical project include these steps:

1. Project kickoff

2. Equipment installation and testing

3. Training

4. Live implementation/cutover

These represent some of the major events or milestones that typically occur. Chapter 5 of this book provides actual recommended milestones for typical projects conducted by banks.

If multiple projects are being conducted simultaneously, it is vital that the major events and milestones be arrayed on the matrix. In this way, items such as training will not be conducted at the same time as other major events.

Once the major events or milestones are determined, they are arrayed across the top of the time matrix as shown in Exhibit 2.11. Care should be taken to restrict the number of milestones to those that are of most importance. The time matrix itself should consist of a single sheet of paper to facilitate easy reading and usage.

Calendar Weeks. The time aspect of this matrix is best illustrated by designing weekly intervals, except in the briefest project, where timeframes may be measured in days. This scale is determined for the entire time window of the project or projects or for calendar dates in general, of the year. Calendar weeks always begin with the Monday beginning that week.

The report itself should reflect an entire quarter, by week. In this way the project manager and others can scan the quarter to determine what major events will be occurring. An entire year can be presented in four consecutive pages.

It is important to note that the calendar weeks indicate only the week in which the event will occur, not the precise date. The actual dates in which major events occur is contained in the project plan. The time

Exhibit 2.11   Major Events on the Time Matrix

Week of	Telephone Training	Microcomputer Project Kickoff	Cabling Completed	Microcomputer Training	Telephone Cutover	Microcomputer Installation

matrix is not designed for absolute precision but to see, at a glance, when these events will approximately occur. An example of the calendar dates and revised subtitles for the time matrix is shown in Exhibit 2.12.

Major Event Completion Schedule. The last and most important part of the time matrix is listing the projected completion of the major events. This is accomplished by reviewing the project plan and ascertaining the targeted date the major event will occur and designating its completion in the week in which it occurs, under the heading of the event. This can be done by shading the box, placing an "X" in the box or, in the case of multiple locations, recording the name of the location at which the event will occur during the week indicated. Once these additions are made, the project manager can array the major events in conjunction with one another to determine whether adequate spacing is provided to ensure adequate time for their completion and/or make adjustments to build in the cushion required. This process is most useful when multiple projects are involved. Exhibit 2.13 provides an example of these completion/activation dates.

Usage

The time matrix is initially developed in "draft" form by the project manager. Once it is determined that no contention exists, the matrix can be finalized. Upon completion, the time matrix is added to the project management tools and used by the project manager to remain up to date with the occurrence of major

Exhibit 2.12   Listing Calendar Weeks and Specifying the Overall Time Period on the Time Matrix

Week of	Telephone Training	Microcomputer Project Kickoff	Cabling Completed	Microcomputer Training	Telephone Cutover	Microcomputer Installation
1-4-93						
1-11-93						
1-18-93						
1-25-93						
2-1-93						
2-8-93						
2-15-93						
2-22-15						
3-1-93						
3-8-93						
3-15-93						
3-22-93						
3-29-93						

Exhibit 2.13   Scheduling Completion Dates for Major Events

Week of	Project Kickoff	Telephone Station Reviews	Telephone Training	System Cutover	Microcomputer Kickoff	Microcomputer Training	Microcomputer Installation
3-1-93	■						
3-8-93		Main Location					
3-25-93					■		
3-22-93		Facility	Main				
3-29-93			Facility				
4-5-93				Main			
4-12-93				Facility			
4-19-93						Main	
4-26-15						Facility	
5-3-93							Main
5-10-93							Facility
5-17-93							
5-24-93							
5-31-93							

events. The project manager literally can view each week and determine what should be occurring.

In addition to this use, the matrix is an effective executive summary report. Along with the Gantt chart, it can be presented to senior management at the start of a calendar quarter to show what major events are occurring and to keep the managers abreast of project status. Most senior executives are not concerned with the detailed activities and steps within a project. Their concern is with major events and milestones, because these represent the culmination of activities and efforts as well as the occurrence of change that will take place in the organization. The time matrix also illustrates the events' impact on the staff and/or customers, which will be of great interest to upper-level managers. For this reason, the time matrix can be delivered to senior managers as well as the project committee and users. A suggested routine is to produce and deliver the project matrix at the start of a new calendar quarter. The project manager should always maintain a working copy of the matrix for the full year. As changes or additions are required, they can be added to the working copy held by the project manager. Changes will occur over time, and the project manager should continue to keep the matrix as up to date as possible.

Finally, the greatest usage for the time matrix is that of a planner. For this reason the project manager should continue to refer to it, "roughing in" new major events to determine how they will relate to other events. In this way, project milestones can occur unimpeded by others; proper use of the matrix provides smooth transitions during major events, for multiple projects.

CRITICAL PATH METHOD (CPM) SCHEDULING

Definition and Purpose

The critical path method (CPM) refers to another type of project management tool. One cannot discuss project tools without making reference to CPM. CPM is a project scheduling mechanism that shows the interrelationships of events and activities based upon activity and event time estimates and duration.

Although CPM is an important project management tool, it is not as frequently used as the project plan or Gantt chart. The reason is its rather cumbersome usability and lack of readability. CPM networks are more complex than Gantt charts and are used for more defined purposes. As its definition implies, CPM is used to show the relationship of events that are to occur in the project process and to emphasize those that must be accomplished in order for the project to be implemented.

CPM can and should be used in conjunction with Gantt charts and most certainly with project plans. The project plan contains the raw information or project instructions that must be accomplished and provides the information that is ultimately displayed in a CPM network.

The basic elements contained in CPM networks are these:

♦ *Events (Nodes):* Events are represented by circles and are the culmination of specific activities that result in the occurrence of a specific event. They are the starting and ending points of activities.

♦ *Activities:* Activities are the actual manifestation of work performed to enable the occurrence of an event. These are represented by lines connecting one event to another.

An example of a blank, simplified CPM network appears in Exhibit 2.14.

CPM networks are useful when multiple projects are occurring concurrently and/or when events depend on one another. CPM highlights which events are critical to the overall completion of the project and identifies the time required, in total, for their completion. The identification of the critical path is an important concept, because it requires the project team to analyze the sequence in which interdependent major events have to occur. "The critical path is the longest path through a project network and determines the earliest date on which work can be completed. It is generally set up to have no latitude."[1]

CPM emphasizes the string of actions that are crucial to the success of the project, in that if any event on this path is delayed or not performed, it impacts the entire project. Whereas other events may be important, they are not critical to the project's overall success.

CPM is used in engineering and science environments more frequently than in the banking industry.

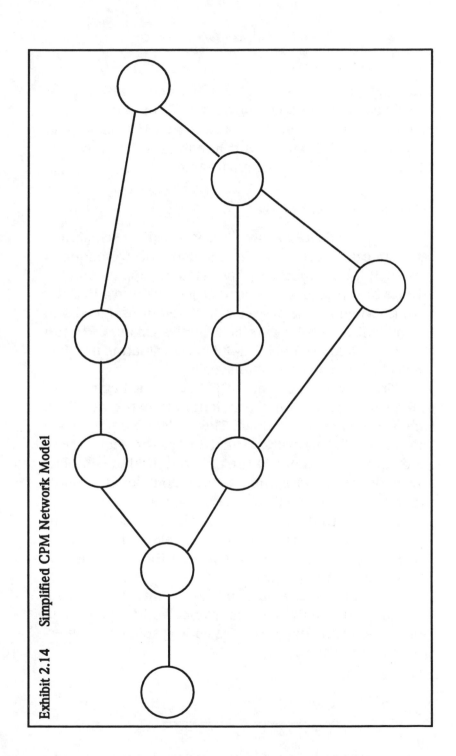

Exhibit 2.14   Simplified CPM Network Model

Its usage is more suited to those fields, although it has bee and can be employed readily in banking. The remainder of this section explains CPM's usage and applicability for banks with attempts to simplify how it might be used in this environment.

Development and Usage

CPM, as its definition implies, is used in scheduling sequence and priorities. In addition, the technique is also helpful in illustrating the relationships among activities and events and thus interdependencies. In other words, when a new project is initiated or assigned and no prioritization of events or activities exists, CPM can be useful. It also can be helpful in coordinating multiple projects occurring simultaneously.

The development of a CPM network begins with the project plan. From this foundation the activities and events are determined. The project manager then uses the CPM network format to set the sequence of activities and ultimately the time required to complete the activities. After setup has been completed, a Gantt chart can be formed, as previously discussed, from the network to display the actual calendar dates. Unlike the Gantt chart, however, the CPM network must be developed as a diagram showing the interrelationships within the project.

Developing the Network Diagram. The first step is to take the activities and events and to code them for usage in the diagram. The coding sequence generally used is this:

Numbers (1, 2, 3....) = Events

Letters (A, B, C....) = Activities

Graphically, an event (or node) is a circle. The activity is represented by a line or arrow connecting it with a prior event. The event represents the starting and ending point of a particular activity or activities. For reference, each event is identified by a number (1, 2, 3 . . .). This aids in describing the flow of events and differentiates them from the actual activity. For bankers' purposes, the activities can be those represented by the major categories or events, in the project plan. Using the events shown in the Gantt chart from Exhibit 2.8, an example of this network is shown in Exhibit 2.15.

Each activity is charted in relation to when the prior item is completed. In some cases, one activity must be completed before another activity can begin. In this sense the process is serial. In other cases two or more activities can occur concurrently, and are not dependent on one another, as in training and installation. These activities are graphically stacked as in Exhibit 2.15, events 5, 6, and 7.

From a project management standpoint, this type of chart demonstrates clearly the order or sequence of activities. Knowing the proper sequence is helpful in scheduling; it indicates which activities must be performed before the others and which can be performed at the same time. This assists the project manager in planning personnel resources and actual timeframes for completion of tasks that overlap. The diagram also

Exhibit 2.15   Coding Activities in Sequence

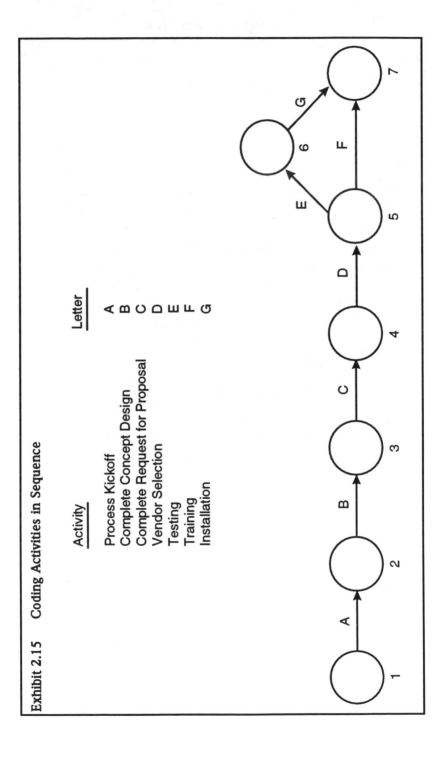

Activity	Letter
Process Kickoff	A
Complete Concept Design	B
Complete Request for Proposal	C
Vendor Selection	D
Testing	E
Training	F
Installation	G

reveals how to trim time from schedules by conducting tasks simultaneously when the path permits.

Time Estimates. Once the diagram is developed, the project committee can develop the time estimates. CPM, as previously stated, is useful for determining the critical path of the project. In the development of the project, however, timeframes must be set in order to assign actual calendar dates as needed in the Gantt chart. This is accomplished by establishing the following estimates:

♦ Earliest start for an activity (ES)

♦ Latest start for an activity (LS)

♦ Earliest finish for an activity (EF)

♦ Latest finish for an activity (LF)

♦ Duration of an activity (D)

Using the standard network diagram, each event (circle) is divided in half to provide room for the earliest and latest start and finishes. Exhibit 2.16 provides an example.

The process of assigning time intervals and timeframes involves three steps:

1. Forward Pass.[2] Each event in the network diagram, moving forward, has the earliest time for each activity established numerically, throughout the whole diagram. In other words, using Exhibit 2.16, a numeric start date is recorded in the first half of the first circle, then more starting dates are added for

Exhibit 2.16   Dividing the Symbols for the Earliest (Left Half) and Latest (Right Half) Dates

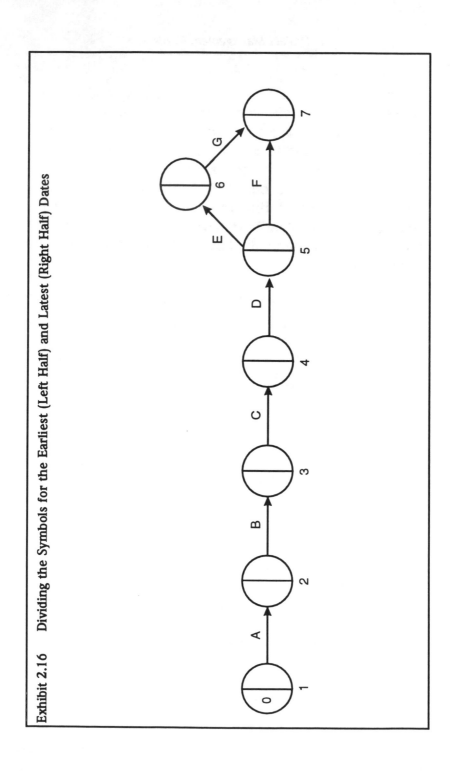

the other events' circles, moving from left to right. Earliest start dates can be either a number (1, 2, 3 . . .), a date (3/18/9X, 3/22/9X . . .) or a Julian date. For simplicity of illustration, working days will be used (0, 1, 2, 3, 4 . . .).

For each activity, the earliest start times are established by referring to the project plan. For each major activity, as in Exhibit 2.15, record the duration of each as the number of days from start to finish. As an example, the duration in calendar days for these activities would be this:

		Duration
1.	Process kickoff	1
2.	Complete concept design	40
3.	Complete the RFP	30
4.	Software selection	25
5.	Testing	35
6.	Training	20
7.	Installation	20

In establishing the duration for activities, working days (total number of days minus holidays and days not worked) should be used.

Each duration period is recorded below the activity arrow, as shown in Exhibit 2.17.

Now the network is ready for the project manager to perform the forward pass. This is accomplished by setting the earliest start dates for each activity. For example, the earliest start date for activity A begins

Exhibit 2.17   Recording Duration Periods in Days under Arrows for Each Event

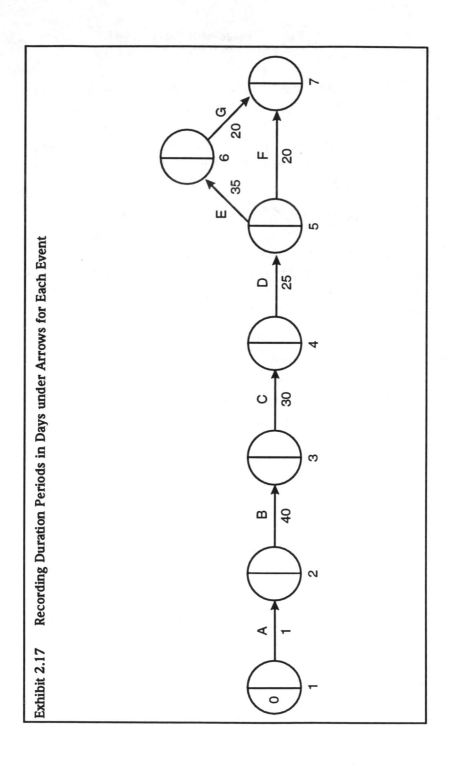

at point 0. Since activity A only requires one working day, the earliest that activity B can start is 1. However, because activity B is dependent on activity A, it can actually be started later as well. Using this approach, earliest start dates for each activity are established, and recorded as in Exhibit 2.18.

When two or more activities route into a single circle (node), the earliest time when the event can be achieved is always the larger of the two, or largest duration of the activities. Earliest starts are also equivalent to earliest finish of the immediately preceding activity. For example, the earliest start for activity C is 41 shown on Exhibit 2.18; this also is the earliest finish for activity B.

2.   Backward Pass Calculations.[3] The next step is to calculate the latest times for each event. This is accomplished, by formula, moving backward from the last event (node) in the project. Latest times are the second hemisphere or right half of the circle.

The first step in this process is to determine the latest time for the final event in the project at node 7. Ideally, the latest time for this event should be equivalent to the earliest time for the event. In the example in Exhibit 2.18, this would be 151. However, as mentioned early in the chapter, the end of the project may be imposed by management. If this is the case, that date must be reflected in the hemisphere in order to perform the backward pass calculations. This example,

Exhibit 2.18   Adding Activity Start Dates for All Events

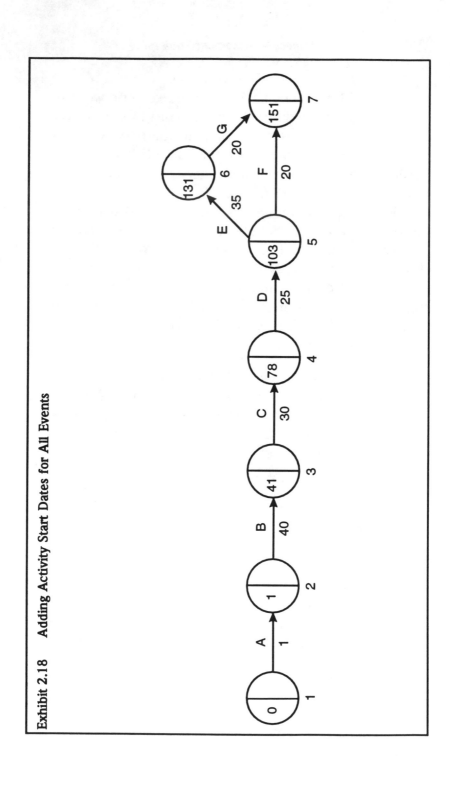

however, used the ideal time of 151 for the latest time.

To perform the backward pass, the following calculation is performed for each activity:

$$\frac{\text{Latest}}{\text{Finish}} - \frac{\text{Earliest}}{\text{Start}} - \text{Duration} = \frac{\text{Maximum}}{\text{Float}}$$

The steps involved in the process are as follows:

1. Assign the latest time for the final event, and record it in the right hemisphere of the circle (in this case, 151).

2. Perform the calculation for the latest activity entering the last node. In Exhibit 2.18, this is activity G. The formula then is:

$$\frac{\text{Latest}}{\text{Finish}} - \frac{\text{Earliest}}{\text{Start}} - \text{Duration} = \frac{\text{Maximum}}{\text{Float}}$$

$$151 - 131 - 20 = 0$$

Because the result of the calculation produced zero, this number is added to the earliest start time of the activity (G) or 131. The result of this addition is 131 (131 + 0 = 131). The number 131 is now recorded in the node, as in Exhibit 2.19, as the latest time.

The result of the calculation is called *maximum float*, the number of days the activity can float between two events. In other words, if the number is positive, more time is available for its completion than the activity actually requires.

Exhibit 2.19   Adding Days to the Nodes During the Backward Pass

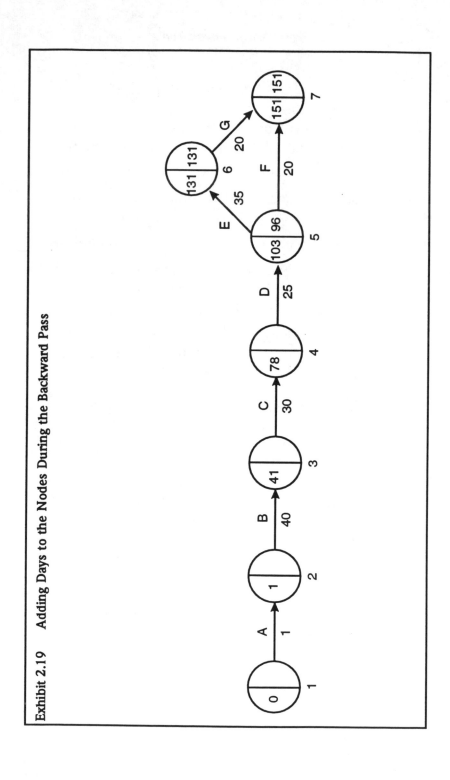

If the result of the calculation is zero (0), there is no float for the activity. Whenever there is zero float, that activity is said to be critical. That is, any change to it will affect the project completion.

In conjunction with this, event six (training) has an earliest and latest time of 131. When the earliest time equals the latest time, the event is said to be a critical event. A critical event is one in which no slack exists. Slack, as will be illustrated, is the difference between the earliest and latest time. Positive slack occurs when the earliest time is greater than the latest time.

Positive slack time means that the event can occur as early as the time indicated and as late as the time indicated without affecting the project completion time. Negative slack, on the other hand, is when the earliest time is less than the latest time. In this case, the event becomes supercritical. As a result, the critical path must be too long and therefore, the supercritical path must be followed.

3.   The same calculation is applied to the next activity, in reverse order, for activity F. Because activity F begins at event 5 with another activity, E, a slight variation in the formula exists.

Whenever two or more activities originate from a single event, the backward pass calculation is:

Maximum float = The lesser or least of:

Latest Time of Activity 1– Earliest Time of Activity 1
– Duration of Activity 1

or

Latest Time of Activity 2 – Earliest Time of Activity 2
– Duration of Activity 2

When this formula is applied, the latest time calculated will be the result of this formula plus the earliest time. Using the previous example, maximum float is calculated as follows, for activities E and F, since they both originate at event five. Lesser of:

Latest Time (E) – Earliest Time (E) – Duration (E) =
Maximum Float (E)

(131   –   103   –   35   =   –7)

or

Latest Time (F) – Earliest Time (F) – Duration (F) =
Maximum Float (F)

(151   –   103   –   20   =   28)

Maximum float, then, is –7 (the lesser of 28 or –7). This then is added to the earliest time in event 5 to calculate the latest time for the event, or 96 (103 + (–7) = 96). This is recorded in event 5 as shown in Exhibit 2.20. Because of the negative float, slack is created at event 5, or rather, negative slack. Because the event has negative slack it is supercritical.[4] This is graphically shown by the bold arrows from events 5 to 6 to 7. The reason for this is that the critical path has zero slack and represents the earliest finish time. If slack is negative, the critical path must be too long, therefore making it supercritical to the project.

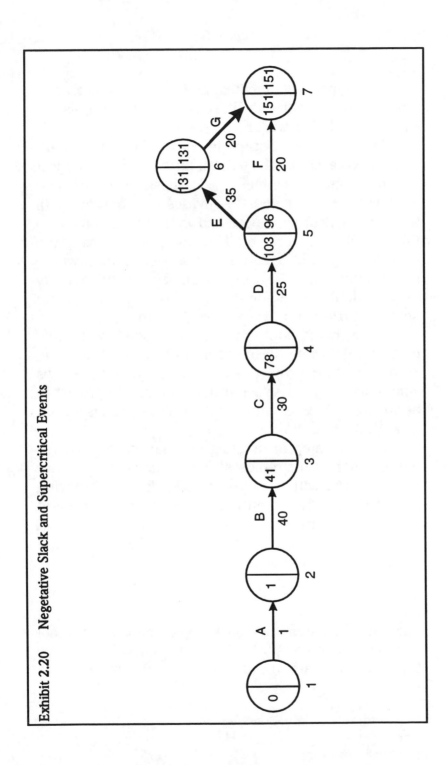

Exhibit 2.20   Negetative Slack and Supercritical Events

The remaining activities and events are then calculated and recorded in this network diagram, as the example in Exhibit 2.21 illustrates.

Critical Path Determination. The critical path as defined earlier is "the longest path through a project network that determines the earliest date on which work can be completed."[5] Activities that have zero (0) float are critical activities, and events that have zero (0) slack are also critical. Therefore, by analyzing the network diagram, it can easily be determined where the critical path is. Beginning from left to right, a heavy bold or double line should be drawn for any critical activity, throughout the entire diagram.

Once this is done, the path can be viewed easily to ascertain what the most important activities and events for the project are. This graphically shows which activities must occur in order for the project to be successful. An example of the critical path is shown in Exhibit 2.22.

The last step is to assign actual calendar dates based on the timeframes shown. This is done either by beginning with a planned start date and moving from left to right or with an assigned end date and moving backward. It is important to keep in mind that times are expressed in *working days*; therefore weekends must be excluded.

Usage

The critical path method as a project management tool can be rather complex. For this reason, it may be beneficial to review a number of software products on

Exhibit 2.21   Adding the Latest Times

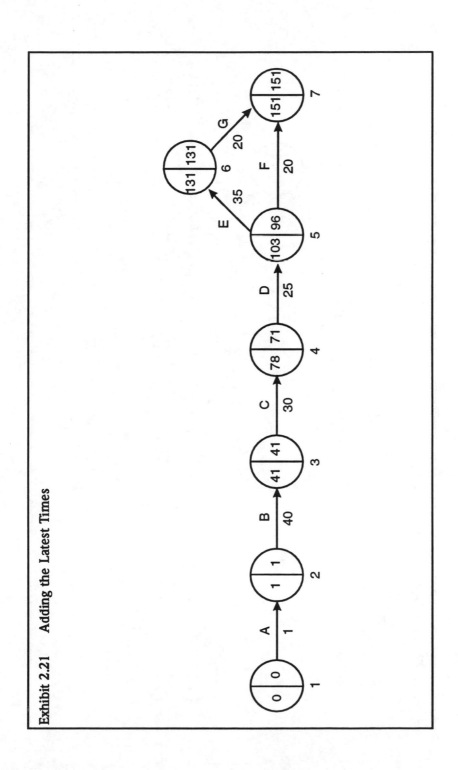

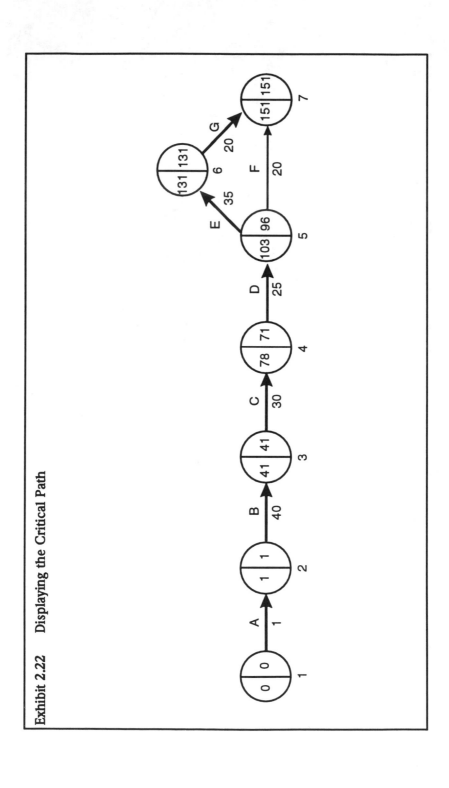

Exhibit 2.22   Displaying the Critical Path

the market that do an excellent job of performing the many calculations and graphically arraying the network. Unfortunately, projects are often quite large. To display all aspects on one piece of paper is nearly impossible unless it is hand developed. For this reason, the previous steps were outlined to provide a means for completing the diagram manually.

For bank project managers the use of CPM is not imperative but can be beneficial for logically determining critical activities and events. This will aid greatly in understanding staffing requirements and other resources for those most important activities. Keep in mind that, if the deadline is important, knowing where attention must be focused, particularly in complex or multiple projects, is vital.

As one might guess, however, the CPM diagram is not very user-friendly. If it is to be used at all, distribution must be limited to the project manager and possibly the project committee. Distributing and displaying this type of information to bank users and senior management is not recommended and could have a detrimental affect on the project as a whole.

Completing major projects requires definite skills for handling a large number and variety of activities at one time. Displaying this graphically to users could psychologically defeat the process before it is started, by overwhelming participants.

In order to be successful in project management, the project manager must have the ability to simplify and break down the large number of tasks and activities into manageable segments. In this way, as segments are completed, they gradually lead to overall project completion. To do otherwise will frustrate users and project team members alike.

Finally, CPM is closely allied with the Performance Evaluation and Review Technique (PERT). The major difference between the two is that CPM relies on experience or historical data for ultimate scheduling. When little or no historical data or experience is available, PERT should be used. PERT emphasizes a statistical determination of earliest and latest times based upon estimates of

♦ Most likely time estimate

♦ Optimistic time estimate

♦ Pessimistic time estimate

The actual data are then statistically calculated to arrive at the earliest and latest times to determine the critical path. Unfortunately, because of the complexity of the statistical calculations it is not feasible to consider using this technique without appropriate software. Once all estimates have been completed, the network diagram is virtually the same as that of the critical path method. Because of this complexity, PERT is seldom used, from a practical standpoint. To emphasize this complexity, PERT first came about as a scheduling method used for the construction of the Polaris submarine jointly developed by the U.S. Navy and Booz, Allen Hamilton in 1958.

For the purposes of this book, no further discussion of PERT is provided. It is not likely that financial institutions will rely heavily on its usage. Most of the needs of banks can be addressed using CPM, even if it must be performed manually. Estimates can be used for time duration and early and late starts to determine the critical path.

Lastly, the primary purpose of both CPM and PERT is the determination of the critical path. Because any activity on this path has zero (0) slack, if the duration exceeds its estimate, the project will also exceed its original targets.

CALENDAR AND TICKLER

Definition and Purpose

Another set of project management tools that can be useful in the process are calendars and ticklers. A calendar is nothing more than an actual calendar (for a month) that indicates what major events will be occurring throughout the month, for the duration of the project. Calendars are generally produced to provide users with a synopsis of events that are occurring. Calendars are similar to the time matrix previously discussed, in that their primary emphasis is the timing of the occurrence of major events. Unlike the time matrix, however, calendars add another dimension, that of the familiar calendar format or layout. The combination of the two elements produces a very user-friendly vehicle for communicating and updating users of upcoming events.

Major events for calendars are milestones in the project process. Recall from earlier discussions that milestones represent significant accomplishments or culminating events worthy of significant note. It is precisely these items that should be highlighted on a major-events calendar. The calendars themselves are monthly—that is, they are a one-page picture showing all days in the month. Specific major events or milestones are indicated by reference to their specific name and/or a bar indicating their occurrence over a period of time. An example of a major-events calendar is displayed in Exhibit 2.23.

Another project management tool used is the time tickler. Time ticklers reduce large volumes of activities into manageable numbers of activities occurring within a given period of time. Time ticklers are project management reports that enable the project manager to see what activities are to be completed this week, without having to find them within the details of the project plan. The purpose of these documents is two-fold. In the first case, the tickler provides a management tracking mechanism for the project manager to monitor which activities are about to occur and to emphasize only those. In the second case, the tickler helps project committee members manage their time more effectively by isolating those activities due. This provides a psychological value to the user because it reduces the volume of work to easily managed numbers.

The time tickler consists of two elements: the "Week of" or time element, and the "Activity Due." Both, where practical, are displayed on a one-page summary report. In addition to this summary, a second page can be developed for all project activities that

Exhibit 2.23   A Blank Major Events Calendar

August 1993
Information Systems Major Event Calendar

Sunday	Monday	Tuesday	Wednesday	Thursday	Friday	Saturday
1	2	3	4	5	6	7
8	9	10	11	12	13	14
15	16	17	18	19	20	21
22	23	24	25	26	27	28
29	30	31				

have fallen past due. This is an effective means of managing a wide variety and volume of activities and tasks for both project manager and users. Exhibit 2.24 gives an example of this report.

Time ticklers serve to condense and to reduce information to manageable quantities and display it in such a way that it provides timely information to the project manager. This report is also shown to project team members and users alike. Again, by condensing data, it serves to focus the individual on the tasks at hand while deemphasizing the voluminous nature of the project activities themselves.

Development

Both reports draw information from the same source; however, the amount and nature of the information displayed are different. The source for virtually all data is the project plan. In this case it is no different. For the major-events calendar, the data required is less detailed and more general. In other words, rather than focus on all the activities associated with and leading up to "training," for instance, the only point of significance is that training is occurring. The following discussion outlines report development.

Major-Events Calendar. Major events must first be determined. This is accomplished by reviewing the project plan and developing a condensed list of major events from all project activities. Major events can be the events (categories of activities) that head each bundle of activities. However, this may prove to be too large to work with. The goal is to develop a short list

**Exhibit 2.24   A Blank Time Tickler: Activities Due This
Week (Above) and Activities Past Due (Below)**

Actual Date	Activity	Responsible

Actual Date	Activity	Responsible	New Target

of events that have significant impact on the project and on the users themselves.

As a rule of thumb, major events will generally consist of the following:

♦ Project kickoff or initiation

♦ Training

♦ Communication

♦ Installation/Implementation

♦ Testing

♦ Process termination

In general, these six items have one thing in common: direct impact on all users. As major events they should be communicated directly to the people involved or affected by the project.

The major-events calendar type of communication is particularly useful when multiple projects are involved. The developer of this report must be careful not to grow this list of major events too large. If too many events are placed on the calendar, it can become cluttered and unreadable. In addition, the types of events recorded must be items that are relatable by the users. If a detailed activity is recorded, the activity itself may have no relation to any one user. If it doesn't, it probably won't be understood, and therefore no one can relate to it. Too many of these on a calendar will cause users to avoid reading it. For this reason, detailed project activities are not included in this report.

With the major events identified, the project manager would review the project plan for the date or dates of its occurrence. These dates are used for display on the calendar. Calendars of this sort are easy to develop, using a variety of software packages that exist on the market. Almost any computer software store can guide the reader to a package that can fulfill these needs. Of course, manual development can be used. However, because the software packages are inexpensive and easy to use, they are highly recommended.

The actual major events, as previously mentioned, are displayed either on the day they occur or as a line or bar showing the span of time required. Unlike the Gantt chart, this report provides actual day-to-day scheduling of events as opposed to tasks spanning weeks. An example of this is shown in Exhibit 2.25.

Time Tickler. Developing a time tickler is different from preparing the major-events calendar. Rather than emphasizing key events or milestones, the time tickler reflects detailed activities, albeit in summarized fashion. Again, the source of the information is the project plan. In this case, however, all detailed activities will be used rather than summarized data.

In order to develop the report, it is necessary to organize the activities contained in the project plan by week—that is, the week that they begin and the week they are targeted to end. A one-page document is used for each week to array what is planned for that week (each page displays its own week). In addition to the exact description of the activity, the individual respon-

Exhibit 2.25   Displaying on the Events and Their Timespans on the Major Events Calendar

May 1993
Information Systems Major Event Calendar

Sunday	Monday	Tuesday	Wednesday	Thursday	Friday	Saturday
						1
2	3	4	5	6	7	8
9	10	11 PC Training	12	13	14	15
16	17	18	19 PC Training	20	21 Telephone Refresher Training	22
23	24	25 Cable Install	26 PC Install Cable Install Star Training	27	28	29
30	31					

sible for its completion is also identified. Exhibit 2.26 provides an example.

As illustrated, the activities recorded have no relation to the general user base. This is the difference between the time tickler and major-events calendar. The items shown are for the project committee and project manager to evaluate and track. In the example, only four activities will be occurring that week, whereas there may be more than 100 activities in the entire project plan. It is psychologically much easier to review a single sheet of paper rather than 15 or 20 at once.

The second page of the time tickler would be "Activities Past Due." This document carries over activities due that were not completed during the week they were targeted to occur. The source of the information is the "Activities Due This Week" report. The

Exhibit 2.26	Displaying Detailed Activities on the Activities Due Report of the Time Tickler

PROJECT
WEEK OF: JULY 12, 199X
ACTIVITIES DUE THIS WEEK

Date	Activity	Responsible
7/12/9X	Begin software development	J. Smith
7/13/9X	Mail RFPs to selected vendors	T. Hart
7/13/9X	Complete installation of hardware	B. Jones
7/16/9X	Develop training schedule	T. Hart

project manager is responsible for keeping this report up to date. Each week, as activities are reviewed, any that are not completed or started as indicated are to be added to the "Activities Past Due" report. Although this page is cumulative, that is, activities can continue to be added to it, it is a forced emphasis of items where targets have been missed, thus forcing a degree of precision to the process. An example of this report appears in Exhibit 2.27.

It is advisable for this type of report to be completed and updated, for distribution, at each committee meeting. This does not have to be weekly. It could be every other week or, at the most, monthly. Preferably the report would be used in conjunction with this meeting. In this way, timely information can be provided and acted upon on short notice.

Exhibit 2.27	Displaying Slippage with the Activities Past Due Report		

PROJECT
ACTIVITIES PAST DUE

Original Due Date	Activity	Responsible	New Target
6/22/9X	Prepare test documents for review	J. Smith	7/22/9X
5/20/9X	Complete the staging of microcomputer hardware	R. Johnson	6/30/9X
7/8/9X	Prepare rough draft of contract	T. Jones	7/15/9X

Usage

The major-events calendar is used by the project manager as a means of communicating with bank users and senior management alike. It is concise and presented in a format that is familiar to the reader: a calendar. This is important because all people involved can relate to the calendar. The communication of this type of information, in this format, is a proactive tactic by the project manager, providing information to the general populace that is likely to affect them. When information of this nature is not communicated, it puts the users in an awkward situation, one that requires them to guess. When users—the ultimate recipients of the project outcome—are left in the dark, it can produce detrimental results. People have a tendency, in this situation, to either assume that the lack of information denotes a lack of control, or that they are not considered important enough to be communicated to. Either way, the project manager does not need this as it can begin to erode or undermine the process. Simply displaying key dates in a familiar format can diffuse much of this misunderstanding. Using the major-events calendar, then, serves to maintain credibility and ultimately confidence.

In contrast to this, the time tickler is not a user document. The time tickler is used strictly as a management tool to better manage and monitor the project process. The audience for this report is predominantly the project committee. It is used during the project implementation committee meetings and is updated based on the frequency of this meeting.

The greatest benefit derived from a report of this nature is its ability to condense the volume of project activities into manageable numbers. It allows project committee members an opportunity to focus on a few items rather than a large volume at once. In addition, the "Items Past Due" aspect allows the project manager to review these as priority items every time the committee meets. In this way, it is less likely that some activities will go uncompleted. Although the project plan itself provides this type of tracking, the time tickler adds another dimension of management that simplifies the process.

Lastly, as an audit tool, these reports represent excellent working papers for documenting what activities remain incomplete at the end of the process. Quite frequently when a project is completed, loose ends remain. Without a means of tracking and highlighting these loose ends they may never be accomplished. Although these items may never have been considered critical or listed on the critical path, if left undone their impact will surface and cause negative repercussions at some point in time. This unprofessional ending can easily be avoided using the calendar/time tickler methodology.

PROJECT TEMPLATE

Definition and Purpose

Project templates are nothing more than standard, boilerplate project activities, preestablished, that can be overlaid on any type of similar process. When a project is introduced in a bank, the project manager and team spend a considerable amount of time determining the detailed steps, timeframes, deadlines, critical paths, and so forth necessary to see the project through to completion. When the project is over, all the time and effort put into it, many times, is lost. When a similar project arises, the information is unavailable and the planning and organizational work must begin again virtually from scratch. This is a considerable waste of time and effort.

Project templates are one way of avoiding the loss of such important information and preserving it so it can be reactivated with minimal developmental effort. All financial institutions have or have had projects that are similar but conducted at different locations. These projects are ideal for project templates and worthy of archiving. Examples of these are mergers and conversions to the same data processor, software development, and major hardware installations and implementations. Each of these projects, once the detailed events and activities have been determined, can be applied or overlaid on other locations or financial institutions requiring those project steps.

Development

Template development and documentation storage is important to the financial institution. If properly developed and stored, the template can be used and refined over and over again. Although this section outlines some of the detail involved in the development of project templates, actual templates used in financial institutions are provided in Chapter 5 of this book.

Templates are easy to develop. Literally, they are the actual project plan and Gantt report that may have been used in the original project, without actual calendar dates supplied. The two primary documents used for template development are the project plan and Gantt chart. Recall from earlier in this chapter that the project plan consists of several elements: event/activities, individual responsible, time interval for completion prior to cutover, beginning/completion targets, actual completion dates, and status. For the development of a project plan template, only the event/activity, individual responsible, and time interval for completion prior to cutover are used. These items provide the shell, or primary elements, needed to re-create the process. Exhibit 2.28 illustrates such primary elements.

The information displayed in this template is taken directly from the actual project plan used in the project, with slight variations.

Event/Activity. The events and activities are those taken directly from the project plan, without variation in most cases. The only time adjustment made is when the activity or event defines or names a specific location. In this case, reference to a particular location should be omitted because the goal is to make the process as generic as possible. In general, however, based on the project type, the events and activities are simply carried over. This is illustrated in the example in Exhibit 2.28.

Exhibit 2.28   Reusable Template for the Project Plan

Event/Activity	Responsible	Weeks Precutover	Time Required for Activity (Weeks)
A. Complete the request for proposal		10	10
1. Determine vendors	Systems Manager	14	10
2. Develop needs list	Systems Analyst	12	5
3. Prepare request for proposal	Director of I.S.	11	5
4. Mail request for proposal	Secretary	10	5

Individual Responsible. Rather than record an actual name, as in the project plan, the template requires only a position title or generic role. The purpose for this is to provide guidance to future project managers and/or future projects to indicate the type of individual who is best suited for performing the activity. Because actual names will change over time, this approach enables the template to be reused easily.

Time Required. The time required is the actual time, expressed in days, required to complete the activity. This is determined from the original project plan. From the project plan's beginning and ending dates, an activity duration can be calculated from the time period. This is then recorded on the project plan template for each activity.

Completion Time Prior to Cutover. The last category of the project plan is the number of days (or time interval) an activity must be completed prior to the cutover or implementation date. This is the same information required in the actual project plan and is simply carried over.

This template can then be stored for later usage.

In addition to the template of the project plan, templates of Gantt charts can also be developed. Although this diagram basically contains the same information, it presents it more graphically. The Gantt chart template is developed from the project Gantt chart recording activities and/or events along the left side of the report. Instead of recording actual calendar (week of) dates across the top of the chart, as in Exhibit 2.9, the dates are replaced with numbers indicating the "week" number prior to cutover or implementation. For developmental purposes, implementation or cutover is always week zero. An example of a Gantt chart template appears in Exhibit 2.29.

As illustrated, the bars are supplied based on the number of days or weeks the activity must be completed in advance of the implementation. The bar is then extended backward the number of days or weeks required to complete the activity. Both items are taken directly from the project plan template. The completed Gantt chart template illustrates the number of days or weeks activities must begin and end and how long they require for completion.

Usage

Project templates are timesavers for recurring projects of an identical or similar nature. Once developed, a template enables the project manager to quickly ascertain specific calendar dates for implementation and project start-up. For example, if the bank president wanted to convert a new acquisition into the group by a given date, the project manager could quickly advise whether this is feasible, and when the project must begin to meet the time deadlines established. The president may learn that the lead time required is not adequate to meet the implementation date desired and that the project must be rethought.

Project templates force a discipline on future projects so that the specific activities have already been identified and the plan itself has proven to be successful. In this way, future projects can be taken on more

Exhibit 2.29   Reusable Template for a Gantt Chart

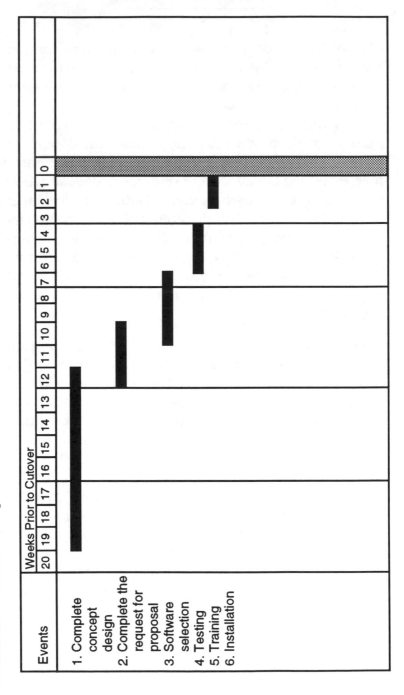

readily without massive effort, up front, to determine the individual tasks and activities.

The Gantt chart template is used by "penciling in" actual calendar dates beginning with the cutover or implementation time. This is always week zero. From this point, dates are recorded in reverse order until the end of the Gantt chart. A review of the start-up of the earliest activity will reveal the date the project must begin to meet the defined implementation date. If this has not already occurred, it is likely that the project can be undertaken. If not, the cutover or implementation must be rethought. In all cases, one must never attempt to condense timelines or activity durations to meet a target date. Doing this will only serve to strain the workload and will likely lead to poor quality and errors.

Of course, if the new project undertaken is of a different nature, the project template may not be of use. However, generic templates can be developed with defined time intervals that can be applied to a wide variety of projects. Examples of this might include computer hardware implementations or new product development. In either case there are always similar elements to complete at specified intervals in advance of cutover. Training is a good example of this. It generally must be completed approximately one to two weeks in advance of cutover regardless of what new system is being implemented. Some generic project templates are provided in the appendix of this book.

SUMMARY

This chapter provided a broad look at a full range of project management tools—their development and ultimate usage.

Of the tools discussed, the project plan is the most critical to any project. Project plans are the slates from which the project instructions and details are recorded. They define the events, activities, individuals responsible, completion time intervals, beginning and ending target dates, actual completion dates, and activity status. These plans are used exclusively by the project committee and are the discussion documents for review of project results and status.

Virtually all projects, once they are approved, must begin with the project plan. Even though other tools may be used to provide some of the data, such as PERT or CPM, the detailed project events and activities are first developed for the project plan. The project plan is seldom used as a communication vehicle for users and senior management, but is a technical blueprint for use by project committee members and other implementors throughout the process.

Gantt charts or timelines were discussed as the second most frequently used project management tool. The Gantt chart presents much of the information from the project plan in a visual format. It is literally a horizontal bar chart indicating project timelines. Gantt charts are less voluminous than project plans and contain less activity detail but more summary-level information. The objective is to reflect the entire project on one page for ease of review and analysis. It typically is used and updated as a "snapshot" of a point in time. The visual nature of the Gantt chart allows for quick and efficient analysis and lends itself well to widespread distribution. Although the project manager and project committee members alike will use the chart, it can and should be directed to senior management and users periodically to demonstrate project progress.

In some cases, additional scheduling tools are required. The time matrix is a chart that provides a means of scheduling events to avoid contention and promote an orderly transition. This document is supplemental in that it is not a primary tool but rather an additional aid that can help plan and schedule multiple events or projects.

The critical path method (CPM) is a scheduling technique that shows the interrelationships of events and activities. One of the most important features of this scheduling tool is its ability to mathematically calculate the critical path, the longest path through the entire project, whereas any change to an event or activity will alter the timeline of the entire project. CPM helps the project manager to better plan resource needs for the completion of activities and to have a good sense of the critical elements of the project. CPM is visual; it is a network diagram that graphically illustrates interrelationships. It is not a user or management reporting tool. Because of the technical nature of this chart, its use is best left to the project manager. For financial institutions, in general, it has limited uses and may not be desired as a project tool.

On the other hand, the discussion of major event calendars provides a tool that can be given directly to users to track various project events. This calendar is familiar to users and unintimidating, providing a strong communication mechanism that would not likely create confusion. Only major events are displayed on this calendar, omitting detailed activities that may have little relevance to the user. In conjunction with this the time tickler is a project management tool that seeks to minimize the voluminous nature of project activities and reduce them to manageable numbers. This report, although easy to read, does focus on the detailed activities. It is designed for project managers and their committees rather than the individual user or senior management. It is helpful in directing attention to activities due or upcoming, to focus attention and gradually work toward a common end.

The last tool discussed was the project templates. After developing a wealth of information on a new project, this approach is a means of capturing and storing the valuable information obtained in a way that allows easy reuse and transition to new projects. Often, projects completed will be run again, at a later date. This is true particularly if they involve generic functions, such as conversion, mergers, system installations, and so on.

This chapter attempted to provide an introduction to a broad array of project management tools, their purpose, definition, development, and usage. In all cases the tools have been tested and proven successful in actual practice. The goal of the chapter was to explain tools that nontechnical managers can apply easily in the banking industry. Efforts were made to simplify the tools' development and usage so a broader audience can benefit from them without intimidation, at little cost, and with maximum understanding.

Project management cannot adequately be performed without some of these tools. It is therefore necessary that the project manager have a good understanding of what is available to him or her. Not only will bank management require this information but it can also provide the project manager with the type of flow and control necessary to ensure that the project is completed on time, on budget, and with minimal disruption to the day-to-day operations of the bank.

NOTES

1. James P. Lewis, *The Project Manager's Desk Reference* (Chicago: Probus Publishing, 1993).

2. Ibid.

3. Lewis, *The Project Manager's Desk Reference.*

4. Ibid.

5. Ibid.

3

Communication
and Control of Projects

PURPOSE AND NEED FOR EFFECTIVE COMMUNICATION

Project management and communication should go hand in hand. In fact, without communication, effective project management cannot take place. This reliance on good communication is not unique in the financial services industry but common across all industries.

In general, the communication necessary in the project management process is directed at four primary areas:

- ♦ Senior management
- ♦ Project committee members
- ♦ Users
- ♦ Customers

Literally, each of these groups is a party to change.

Senior Management

When a project is undertaken, it is usually approved—or at the very least, endorsed—by senior management. Because senior managers are generally the group that commits the funds necessary to see the project through, they are a primary communication point throughout the process. As Chapter 2 stressed, senior management communication is vital, but it must be in a format that provides the maximum benefit with the least amount of effort. Senior executives have little time, as well as little patience, for voluminous detail. When communications longer than a page are directed to them, their level of attention begins to wane. Nevertheless, communication of project progress must occur. Devising effective communication to upper management is somewhat of a dilemma: If too much detailed information is provided, it can be the same as no information, because it will not be read. Senior management, then, is left to guess what the project status is.

As a general rule, for project management purposes, the communication to be delivered to senior management should contain the following traits:

♦ Regular communications

♦ Timely communications

♦ Concise communications

Although the types of communication mechanisms will be illustrated later in this chapter, the meaning of each type is explored more fully here.

Regular Communications. *Regular* means occurring at a predetermined time without deviation. In other words, once the pattern of communication is established, it should continue without fail. Not only does this make communications easier to schedule but enables the project manager to plan the communication effectively, remaining in control of it, rather than being questioned by upper managers on an impromptu basis. Regularity builds confidence as well as orderliness in the process. This enables senior management the time to formulate their questions, in advance of regularly scheduled meetings, to gain comfort and confidence in the process.

When possible, the project manager should discuss with senior management the regular nature of the communications early in the project, or even before the kickoff meeting begins, to establish the interval. In this way, the orderliness of the communications becomes part of the overall process.

Timely Communications. *Timeliness* refers to the frequency and timing of meetings—in other words, when the communications are delivered. Is the frequency every week, every other week, monthly, or quarterly? When the project manager determines the timeliness of communications, obtaining feedback from senior managers about how often is enough is most beneficial and highly advised. Every CEO or other senior manager has different requirements for what is timely. When a project manager guesses at this or assumes he or she knows what the bank CEO wants, he or she is likely to err. This misjudgment can be detrimental to the project. Rather than take the risk, it is best to find out exactly what senior management prefers and then proceed accordingly.

When the actual timeliness of communications is determined, the responsibility and schedule for the communications should be worked into the project plan to ensure their timely occurrence. Once this is done, it is the responsibility of the project manager to ensure that communications are conducted as planned.

As a final note, regardless of the feedback received from the regular communications, the project manager should never deviate from the schedule. If senior managers do not respond, this should not be taken as an indication of their lack of concern. If the communications are not taken seriously and become sporadic, the project manager begins to lose control of the communications and therefore, allows senior management to guess or interpret the meaning of such infrequency. Usually the result isn't positive.

Concise Communications. Regardless of the type of communications, they must be concise. Bank CEOs and other senior executives have little time to read a project plan. Therefore, communications must be reduced to those key elements that senior management can relate to and understand, usually major events or milestones that highlight significant events. Actions falling into these categories include training, actual installation of equipment, contract negotiations and execution, project kickoffs, and communications to users and customers. All of the items mentioned have one thing in common, from a CEO standpoint: an impact on bank personnel. Whenever projects begin to affect the workforce of the bank or its customers, senior executives of the bank want to know about it. By limiting the communications to the status of such major events and categories, the project manager can effectively keep senior management aware of the project status and not lose their interest.

Communications to senior management can be effective if these simple rules are kept in mind. The only question remaining is the type or form of communication most appropriate. It is probably unlikely that a verbal or face-to-face communication will occur with the frequency desired. Therefore, the project manager must be prepared to deliver the most effective type of printed communication. In this sense written or visual communications cannot be avoided.

Although written communications are effective if concise, discussion of this topic will be deferred until later in the chapter. Visual (graphical) communications, however, will likely have a place in paper-based communications. This type of communication, to senior management, is outlined in great detail in Chapter 2, "Project Management Tools," of which the most effective reporting mechanisms, are

♦ Gantt charts

♦ Time matrices

♦ Calendars

Any of these three will fit the criteria for capturing senior managers' attention. To explore which type to use, review Chapter 2.

Although it's hard to go wrong with effective written or visual communications, the project manager is wise to present the reporting options to senior management to determine whether those managers have a preference, and to provide some preliminary familiarity with the report formats. In addition, this discussion will establish the format, whether it be totally written, visual, or oral.

When the project progresses to the installation/implementation stage, however, verbal communication is a must as a reminder of the major events to follow. No matter how concise a report is, the CEO may have other issues on his or her mind at the time of project implementation. The project manager should not leave it to the written reports to communicate the big event. A timely call, placed in advance of a cutover, is a prudent and courteous action to take to draw attention to the event.

Committee Members

Because of their detailed responsibility to execute the plan, the type of communication necessary for project committee members' success will differ from that of senior managers. Although their communication means, at a minimum, must be regular and timely, it can occur more often than that designated by the project manager. Committee members are doing the tasks; therefore, they are very closely involved with the detail of the project, whether working with sub-committees or simply performing the work themselves.

Much of the communication occurring with committee members originates from the project committee meeting. The various parts and aspects of this meeting are discussed later in this chapter. The communication that occurs at meetings is verbal and written, emphasizing project detail. Literally, for each major event or milestone there are myriad tasks and activities to be performed. Project committee members perform these tasks directly or indirectly. As a result, the information required is in the detailed format of the project plan. In other words, the detail they require is virtually the day-to-day communications necessary to meet the timeframes established in the project plan. When the committee comes together on a regular basis in the project committee meeting, the written reports will be most beneficial and used by them will be

♦ The project plan

♦ Gantt charts

♦ Time ticklers

These three project management tools are all likely to be useful to the committee. Each document is updated for communication at the next committee meeting. For a detailed discussion of the development and usage of these tools refer to Chapter 2.

Finally, project committee member communications are constant throughout the process, to and from the project manager, and one another. Because many activities are occurring simultaneously, issues of scheduling will arise. The forum that provides the interaction among project committee members and the airing of such issues is the project committee meeting.

Users

Obviously, one of the major groups requiring communication are the beneficiaries of the project outcome, the users. Users are employees of the bank who will actually operate the new system, hardware, software, or new products or procedures delivered by the project committee. In most cases, users represent the reason the project was undertaken—to either improve a given process or provide more information to the workforce.

User communication can be somewhat complex because many people are involved. Furthermore, because they are the recipients of the project outcome, they are the individuals who will be changed the most by the process. As a result, the project manager and committee may ultimately be faced with fear, apathy, and outright hostility. Unfortunately, this ambivalence exists because users compose the one group that usually has the least amount of input in the process at its inception. Unlike senior managers, who have requested or authorized the project, and the project manager who is completing the project, users have little choice but to wait until their work lives are changed at the end of the process. The project manager must be acutely aware of these sensitivities, because this will be the most emotional of the three communication groups discussed thus far.

Depending on the project scope, the user base affected could be narrow or it could be companywide. In the latter case, communication timeliness and regularity become major issues. If the bank is large and regular communications are desired, it can be very disruptive to daily work to disseminate written communications with any frequency. Furthermore, to provide written communications often may be cost prohibitive. How then are users kept informed?

The path to successful communications to users is through the supervisors and managers who manage them. This is absolutely critical to the process and many times overlooked by senior and project management alike. Department managers and supervisors are typically caught in the middle of the process. They may not have had any initial input in determining why the project is needed or should be undertaken. They may not be directly affected by it, even though their staff members will be. This places the department managers in a situation where they have little control. The decision to proceed is made by senior management. Project management and committees will complete it, and the employees will use it. Where then do the middle and line managers fit in? As managers, having little control over the process violates the nature of their role in the organization. In fact, their very role is control of their department and the work performed there. When something occurs that affects that control, there will always be a conflict if it is something in which the manager has little involvement or communication. Therefore, the key to success for user communication is not directly to the staff affected, but rather to their managers and supervisors, and then to them.

To that end, it is advisable to communicate with managers regularly, enabling them to understand the changes that will occur and buy into them. Once this occurs, the managers can communicate the changes to their staff in the normal course of business.

A major lesson to be learned in any project is that although users can easily be trained, if their direct supervisor does not know how to manage the new system, it will not be used, or at least it will not be used properly. User communications, then, begin with departmental supervisors and managers. The types of communications required for this group are different from the others and must consist of the following types of information:

♦ Content-based

♦ Event-driven

Content-Based Information. Regular communications are less important than timely communications, for this group. However, line managers must be made aware of:

♦ What the project outcome will involve

♦ What the benefits of it will be

♦ How it will be managed

In other words, content is of most importance. Rather than emphasizing only when various activities and events will be completed, communications should make line managers aware of what the impact will be on them and their staff members' work lives. Furthermore, the managers must be helped to see what positive benefit the project will have for them. In short, these managers require information that will enable them to become comfortable with the outcome. This comfort level is vital, because if the managers are uncomfortable or unknowledgeable of the impact and benefit, they can't manage to attain it. If managers are left in the dark and unconvinced, this suspicion will transfer to their employees with detrimental results. If these line managers do not consider the innovation important and/or do not know how to manage it their employees will be on their own. If the situation reaches this point, any amount of direct communications to the users themselves will be a waste of time, because the message will not be reinforced.

Again, the key to successful user communications is through their direct line managers. The project manager can best accomplish this verbally by conducting timely sessions, with the group, early in the project process well before users begin to learn about it through the grapevine. The worst case would be to delay these sessions until well into the project, when the company grapevine is in high gear. When the information void occurs, employees will go to their immediate bosses to clarify any of their concerns. If the line managers are not prepared to field these questions, they have been placed in an awkward position. Line managers must be proactive with their staff. That is, when changes are about to occur it is always best to hear it first from the direct superior who can usually lend perspective to the issue and smooth its transition. Without this, distrust and rejection of the project goals occur.

These communication sessions should be content heavy and, where possible, include live demonstrations. Remember, this group must buy into the process and fully grasp it in order for the innovation to be successful. In this way, the line managers can communicate the amount of content information they feel is necessary for their employees to be prepared for the change. They will know best what exactly their employees need.

Event-Driven Information. The second type of communication is event-driven information. This relates to the classical aspects of the project; the timeframes and events occurring. Managers and their employees can both be kept informed of the major events occurring through written or visual materials. Like senior management, both line managers and users do not require a great amount of project detail. What they do require, however, is the major events that will most directly affect them. The events that typically will affect them are: training, actual installation/implementation, and project preparation. This can easily be accomplished with either of the following project management tools:

♦ Time matrix

♦ Major-events calendar

The time matrix will be a valuable tool for the line manager to learn which major events affect his or her employees, in relation to other events occurring. This will help the manager to schedule more effectively and to provide information to project management where overlap or contention may exist. The time matrix should originally be prepared by the project manager and submitted to the group, early in the process, for comment.

The major-events calendar is a user-friendly tool that can be prepared for the entire month showing upcoming events, making it a good communication mechanism directly to the user. If properly communicated through their line manager, the calendar will ease users' transition to the new system. Both the time matrix and major events calendar are discussed in detail in Chapter 2.

In conclusion, users compose an important section of communication. The project manager should never underestimate the need to communicate to this group and the methodology needed to do it effectively.

Customers

Virtually every project undertaken will have some effect on external customers. Even if the bank has taken on only a project to upgrade its teller system, for instance, that new approach will impact the customer in faster service or more expanded service. When this change occurs, regardless of how subtle the change is, the customer is impacted. Although it is discussed last in the sequence here, this group should be considered well in advance of the project completion.

In general, the most common reasons for undertaking projects usually is driven by customers' needs. Whether that need is additional information, more service, improved communications, or better technology, the bottom line is that customers will be affected. Even when a new system is developed to streamline an operational function, the customer is still affected. Improved productivity translates into more time saved and lowered cost to perform the function, which in turn can be passed along to the customer.

Because most projects affect the customer in some way, albeit subtly, an opportunity is created. This is an opportunity to sell the organization in the way it is becoming state of the art, is continually improving, or simply is acting on customers' suggestions. All of these motivations for change should be shared with customers to create a net benefit to the bank by way of improved client relations. The important concept to be grasped is that change, achieved through new projects, affects more than the bank staff; customers must also be considered. The communication to customers can take two forms:

♦ Informative/instructive

♦ Marketing

Informative/Instructive. When a project is completed that has obvious effects on the customer, such as a voice response system, a new interactive teller machine, or modernized lobby layout, the customer must be informed in advance of the change. This is simply good business. If a bank changes the way it does business it had better inform and, in some cases, train its customers; otherwise, the institution will lose business. An example of this is the "trainer" ATMs that some banks use to instruct customers in teller machine operation and subsequently reduce the fear of its usage.

If the bank's customer service line is now answered by a machine prompting the customer to press various buttons to obtain service, the institution had better prepare customers in advance for this major change in service. This will only serve to minimize disruption, dissolution and ultimate loss of accounts.

Marketing. When a project has subtle impact to the customer, such as a new teller system that allows for more efficient transaction handling, an opportunity exists. The opportunity that is available is pure marketing—that is, selling the bank to its customers for embarking on projects that will improve not only operations but service to them as well. A new teller system could go unnoticed by customers; however, if properly marketed, it could draw the customers' attention to the fact that they were in and out of the line faster, received much simpler receipts, or were able to be recognized without requiring identification at the window.

When customers are told, in advance, of the impact of a new system, the message creates an awareness and an impression. If the communication is properly done, the impression will be positive and the customer will become part of the process. The major complaint of any bank customer are changes that simply appear, with seemingly little thought of customer convenience and without feedback from them. By performing these communications early, the bank can diffuse customer negative responses and literally reverse the impression.

Unlike the other groups, the communication mechanisms used for customers do not fall under the standard project management tools. Such communications would be public relations efforts for customers. The province of customer communications is marketing and customer relations. However, the basic information required must be obtained from the project manager. For this reason, marketing and customer relations personnel should work closely with the project manager to determine the impact of the project on customers and whether an opportunity exists to improve the institution's public image.

The type of data necessary for customers is bottom line—customers want to learn what the change does for them and why it's a benefit. Carefully analyzing this relationship will go a long way toward enabling the marketing staff to develop the type of communications that will be of considerable interest to the customer.

MANAGING CHANGE

Early on, this book referred to managing change and the psychological effect it has on people. The previous section focused on a need to carefully communicate with a variety of groups. Although this may seem fundamental, it isn't. Once projects begin it is relatively easy to become so focused on tasks as to forget communications. This happens frequently, so it deserves special mention.

Change is difficult for all parties to the process, from senior managers through to the customers. When communication occurs regularly, and frequently, it has a positive psychological effect on everyone, which allows the people affected to gradually understand and accept or even embrace the change. This is much preferred to the "head crashing" effect of an overnight change. When this occurs there is no time to adjust, to understand, and to assimilate the change into your frame of reference.

Much can be learned from experience and by doing. Analyzing personnel impact will help the project manager to intuitively know when communication is necessary and beneficial. It should become a part of his or her repertoire of tools to use in affecting an orderly transition. The bottom line is

"Communicate, communicate, and
communicate."

The final section of this chapter is devoted to the mechanics of project committee communications and the importance of the project committee meeting.

THE PROJECT COMMITTEE MEETING

Project committee meetings are the glue that keeps the process together. It is a sort of general governing body that comes together to analyze the process, pro-

gress, events and even problems that may have occurred. The project committee meetings serve as a
forum for regular communication of all parties directly
involved in the project: the project committee and
project manager, as defined in Chapter 1.

The committee meeting serves as a forum to bring
together the issues and concerns that arise during the
process. Throughout the course of a project, issues
arise for which no specific answers or direction exists.
Without the committee meeting, the resolution of such
issues is left to local wrangling. This may not conform
with the overall mission and scope of the project. To
prevent this, the committee meeting provides an airing
ground where the issues can be raised and discussed,
and participants can outline the direction necessary
for resolution from a common viewpoint. In addition,
it is a way for all project committee members to come
together and check the status of the variety of project
activities in process.

In short, the project committee meeting is as vital
to the process as the project plan itself is. This section
outlines how the committee is composed as well as
how it functions.

Committee Participants

As a general rule, the project committee is composed
of all project team members. The committee is facili-
tated and chaired by the project manager, who reports
directly to the senior management group in the organization who has authorized the project. During the
life of a project, many people are involved in the actual

completion of the activities. These activities may be delegated by the committee member responsible for their completion, as defined in the project plan. It is not necessary for those to whom the work is delegated to attend the regular committee meeting, unless their presence is requested for clarification and understanding. It is the role of the responsible project committee member to voice any concerns raised by the individuals performing the activities. In this way, the committee remains at a manageable size and can address all the issues surfaced as well as review project progress.

In the early stages of the project, the committee will likely be smaller than it will be toward the project's end. At the onset, some of the control committee members, such as representatives from training and communications, may not need to be fully involved. Because control members represent support areas, their contributions should not be called upon when little is occurring involving their area of expertise. The project manager is the facilitator and therefore advises when it is appropriate for the various control members to participate.

Functional members, on the other hand, generally participate in committee meetings throughout the process. The reason is that they are the users or the persons most impacted by the project's outcome. In addition, they represent the primary workforce for accomplishing the activities. Functional members must be involved in all issues of the process in order to ensure that all concerns are adequately addressed.

Although senior management is welcome to attend, it is unlikely that a senior bank officer will be present at regular committee meetings. Committee meetings are quite detail-oriented, and such details are usually of little interest to senior executives. However, it may be necessary from time to time to solicit involvement from a senior decision maker when issues are raised of a global nature that may have considerable impact on the bank. In this case, a decision may be required. The project manager must make this assessment and involve senior officers as the situation warrants.

The Kickoff Meeting

The project kickoff meeting is somewhat of an event in the life of a project. It is akin to "opening day" in baseball and is the launching pad from which the formal process is begun.

Attendance at the kickoff meeting is the largest of any session during the entire life of the project. Not only are all functional members in attendance but all control committee members as well. The CEO and other senior level officers who have initiated the project should be there. Often these individuals are asked to address the committee to begin the process. This keynote address is highly recommended and should outline, to the committee, the following:

♦ Management's endorsement of the project

♦ The reasons for its undertaking

♦ The project's importance to the bank

- ◆ The benefits the project will provide to the bank

- ◆ The empowerment of the project manager and committee to coordinate its completion

It is important to require attendance at the kickoff committee meeting. If done properly, the message imparted by the meeting provides impetus for the project initiation and fuel for its launching.

The kickoff meeting sets the tone for the project and legitimizes the process. Without it, projects flounder without the necessary credentials and blessings needed to venture forward. The agenda for the project kickoff committee should consist of the following:

- ◆ Introductions and reasons for the meeting

- ◆ Keynote address

- ◆ Project scope

- ◆ Project personnel composition

- ◆ Project plan

- ◆ Project timelines

- ◆ Project meeting frequency

- ◆ Project benefits

- ◆ Initial project meeting

- ◆ Next meeting schedule

- ◆ Adjournment

This agenda is developed and circulated by the project manager. Although many agenda items exist, the purpose is to provide an overview of each area so as to provide a good understanding of all aspects of the project. This is accomplished in an executive summary format, because many of the participants may be senior managers. The explanation of these agenda items are expanded on here.

Introductions and Reasons for the Meeting. The first order of business is to identify the project. Generally, a name is developed that identifies the project, often in the form of an acronym. This identification acknowledges to all the parties to the project that they are where they should be as expected.

Because this meeting is relatively large, the second order of business is to provide introductions for everyone in attendance. This is usually accomplished by going around the room, announcing names and titles of everyone in the group. CEOs, senior executives, or other special attendees should be separately identified by the project manager. Other special attendees could be consultants, vendors, or other nonbank personnel involved in the process.

Keynote Address. Following the introductions, the project manager would introduce the CEO or senior officer to address the group. The keynote address enables the audience to understand management's involvement, commitment, and endorsement of the project. It provides a good initiation of the process and requisite motivation necessary at the beginning.

Project Scope. The project scope is discussed by the project manager as the boundaries within which the project will operate. This defines what the project will and will not do. It establishes an expectation level for the outcome of the project so that false or misleading expectations do not occur.

Project Personnel Composition. The actual project committee is defined as the players who will be involved in seeing the project through to completion. This will require the identification and introduction of both functional and control project committee members who will be involved in the process. In addition, consultants or outside third parties who might also be involved would be introduced at this point.

Project Plan. The project manager distributes and reviews the project plan with the kickoff group. The purpose of this is to highlight what is involved in the process. Emphasis is placed on major categories or events rather than detailed activities. In this way the kickoff committee will understand the breadth of the project.

Project Timelines. A Gantt chart illustrating key project dates is circulated and discussed. The project manager should draw attention to specific dates of all major events, to include: training, testing, and actual cutover. This is one of the most important aspects of the kickoff meeting, and creates an awareness and understanding of the times in which events will occur.

Project Meeting Frequency. The timing and scheduling of all project committee meetings is outlined to set the level of commitment required of these members. This also provides a sense of control for all attending individuals so that they become comfortable with how it will be monitored.

Project Benefits. Finally, what the project outcome will produce by way of benefits is analyzed. This overview explains to the committee and senior management how the project will affect them and how it will hopefully improve their current process and procedures.

This typically is the last part of the full kickoff meeting. Once completed the CEO, senior executives, and other noncommittee members may adjourn.

Initial Project Meeting. The remaining individuals should be the nucleus of the ongoing project committee. At this stage, a brief meeting is held to outline what activities are due, to begin the process, and to hold a discussion of any relevant issues or concerns. The standard committee meeting format is observed, as will be discussed in the next few pages, although in an abridged form.

Next Meeting Schedule. The next project meeting date is established as well as forthcoming meetings and schedules.

Adjournment. The kickoff meeting is formally adjourned.

Project Committee Meeting Frequency

The ongoing project committee meetings should be conducted on a regular basis at regular intervals. Typically, project meetings are best conducted every other week. This frequency provides enough time for activities to be completed, but at an interval that maintains close monitoring so as not to jeopardize key project completion targets.

Early in the project life, the project manager should assess the project plan for initial activity completion. At the start, project committee meeting frequency could be as much as three weeks apart. This allows time for work to be performed without burdening project committee members with administrative meetings. As the project moves toward midlife, every-other-week update meetings are necessary. Again, this allows more timely monitoring and communications to avoid deviations from completion targets that go uncommunicated until it is too late to do anything, jeopardizing the overall project target completion date.

As the project moves into the final phase, the weeks before cutover, it is highly advisable to conduct project committee meetings weekly. This is a crucial time in the project's life and one during which any slippage in activities can literally set back the entire project. In addition, as the project nears the cutover week, more issues are raised that require quick resolution than before. Due to human nature, as deadlines near, there is a heightened sensitivity and greater sense of urgency. Weekly meetings should continue through cutover, until most of the major issues have been resolved.

Although formal meetings occur on the scheduled basis the project manager should advise the committee that urgent issues should not wait until a formal meeting. In this case it is important to emphasize directing these issues to the project manager as they occur, to avoid delaying a critical activity or event.

Project Committee Meeting Format

The format of the project committee is designed for maximum control and coverage of project detail. To that end, the recommended sequence of events is a proven method for addressing most of the detail that will occur.

Managing larger projects can be a considerable job. As such, structures and mechanisms must be in place to ease the burden of management while preventing the omission of activities and events. The project committee meeting is one method for garnering that type of control. The key to project committee meetings is repetition and order, bordering on the obsessive level. To ensure this type of control the format of the meetings should always consist of the following:

1. Review of the project timeline Gantt chart

2. Review of the project plan, and activities due and past due

3. Review of outstanding issues raised from the last meeting contained in the meeting minutes

4. Discussion of new issues

Each project committee meeting must focus on these four aspects religiously, at each session. This ensures that very little is missed or unaccounted for. Unlike the regular management of a department everything that is involved in a project has a definite time when it must be accomplished. The committee meeting, therefore, serves as a formal tickler to monitor the items and ensure that they are accomplished. Further explanations of the four parts of the meeting format follows:

♦ *Project timeline review:* This is performed by the project manager, drawing everyone's attention to the Gantt chart. This review is necessary to emphasize the timeline and put the current time into the perspective of the project timeline. Psychologically, it forces committee members to be cognizant of where they are in the project timeline, how far or near to cutover they are, and what major events are coming up.

   The review itself is brief—merely an overview of where the project is at that point in time. Emphasis is placed on how far from cutover the current date is and which events/activities are worthy of attention.

♦ *Project plan review:* The next phase of the meeting is the review of the project plan. This is a more time-consuming review, because the project manager reviews each of the detailed activities coming due. The review itself is a discussion of each activity, requiring a status update from the committee member responsible for it. As project activities are completed, the project manager makes notations to the plan for update.

Chapter 2 showed examples of the project plan and its subsequent development. Exhibit 2.5 illustrates a developed project plan. As activities are completed, the project manager must update the plan to record the actual completion date and status of the activity. In most cases, the status section contains the word *complete.* This column of the project plan, as illustrated in Exhibit 3.1, is used for this purpose or to record any other message needed for documentation purposes. As the example shows, other messages can be supplied, such as "Deferred" or "Not Applicable." When the manager uses messages, they should be limited to one or two words for simplicity and ease of review. This simplicity will only speed the review of project plans.

It is important to update the project plan regularly (before each committee meeting). Not only does the plan provide a trail of work completed but also a psychological value and a sense of accomplishment for getting things done. Never ignore this opportunity. Although project committee members are typically stoic and task oriented, they are nevertheless human and can benefit by the positive feedback.

In addition to activities due or coming due, the project plan shows the activities that have not been accomplished as targeted and are therefore past due. These, too, are discussed. Each project committee member should be prepared, in advance, to respond to their area of responsibility during this portion of the meeting.

♦ *Review of meeting minutes from the last meeting:* In addition to activities that must be ac-

Exhibit 3.1   Adding Completion Dates and Status Notes to the Project Plan's Status Column

Event/Activity	Responsible	Weeks Precutover	Target Begin	Target End	Actual End	Status
A. Complete the request for proposal	J. Smith	10	3/08/93	4/19/93		
1. Determine vendors	R. Jones	14	3/08/93	3/22/93	3/25/93	Complete
2. Develop needs list	T. Jenkins	12	3/22/93	4/05/93	4/07/93	Complete
3. Prepare request for proposal	J. Smith	11	4/05/93	4/12/93		Delayed
4. Mail request for proposal	P. Roberts	10	4/12/93	4/19/93		

complished from the project plan, committee members will also raise issues, problems, concerns, and decision points relative to the process and activities. These are documented in the meeting minutes. After the project plan review is completed, this is the next phase. Analyzing the issues raised during the last meeting will enlighten everyone about their resolution or ongoing concern. In this way, project issues are raised and addressed on a timely basis rather than lingering until they become critical at cutover, or never addressed.

♦ *New issues discussion:* The final phase of the meeting is the discussion of any new issues, problems, concerns, or decision points that have arisen since the last meeting. It is important to document these in the minutes for review at later meetings. Issues are important parts of the project process. No project plan can address every aspect that will arise; therefore, a forum must exist for handling new twists as they surface. This is one of the primary purposes of the project committee meeting. By raising the issues for discussion, all committee members can comment and come to understand how the turn of events affects them and whether they need to provide input.

Following this format at every meeting will guarantee a successful process and transition. It literally is a disciplined approach for controlling information and activities within tight time constraints. This kind of discipline is necessary, because once the process is begun it is difficult to stop, go back, or alter its path. If discipline is lacking, the members and project manager alike will be running behind throughout the entire process.

Meeting Facilitation

Although a high degree of structure and control is involved in project committee meetings, they nevertheless require skill and finesse in order to guide their direction. The project manager is the facilitator or chairperson of the committee. Facilitation requires the ability to perform the following in the meeting setting:

- ◆ Control the meeting
- ◆ Move the meeting forward to stay within time boundaries
- ◆ Order responses and activity completion from committee members (delegate)
- ◆ Know when to escalate issues
- ◆ Demonstrate organizational skills

These criteria for effective project committee meeting facilitation are a must if the project manager and the project are to be successful. It is easy, given the volume of activities and events and the diverse group represented by the committee members, for committee meetings of this sort to get out of hand or become nonproductive. If the meeting is noneffective, committee members will lose faith in the process and will be unwilling to attend. If this were to occur, there would be no formal management of the process and issues would go unsurfaced or poorly addressed. The only result can be project failure.

As was outlined in Chapter 1, the selection of a project manager is quite important. The individual must not only have the ability to manage people over whom he or she has no legitimate authority but also must have the ability to meet the criteria for conducting effective project committee meetings, as elaborated here:

♦ *Control of the meeting.* Because of the nature of the issues discussed in the project meeting, it is relatively easy for discussions to become heated and for members to become sidetracked. This invariably will occur because of the discipline and detail involved. The project manager must be able to "rein in" the group and refocus the members on the important points to resolve them appropriately. Unfortunately, not all issues can be resolved immediately, at the table. Some require escalation, deferment, or simply more research. It is the role of the project manager to listen critically and direct or redirect the conversation to its logical end. Remember, time is the major factor for projects and project meetings. It is always limited. Therefore, time must be used effectively so that decisions can be made and action taken as required.

Although the project manager may not have the technical expertise to perform the activity or activities at issue, he or she must be able to grasp the important issues and direct the discussion.

♦ *Move the meeting forward to remain within time boundaries.* Committee meetings that last more than two hours begin to break down. Because of the intensity and detail involved, people become mentally fatigued at some point and begin to "tune out." When this occurs, the meeting will no longer be productive and any decisions made may be suspect. A good project manager must be able to set expectations for meeting duration and attain them. This type of control and sensitivity to time will lend a sense of crispness to the process and will capitalize on the energies of everyone present. When the energies begin to wane, the meeting should end. It is for the project manager to sense this and to be in tune with the committee and the level of quality that flows from it.

Given the structure of the meeting, the project manager should establish timeframes for each segment and remain within these time intervals. The effective time management of the meeting will lend credibility to the process and to the project manager alike, thus creating positive expectations on the part of the project team.

♦ *Orderly responses and activity completion from committee members (delegate).* Because few formal reporting relationships exist between the project manager and committee members, the project manager must be astute in the process of delegation. During the course of the meeting, the project manager must solicit commitment from members for specific time-frames to complete activities. This is not a simple process, especially because no formal authority exists over the committee member. In addition to soliciting time commitments, the project manager must also delegate responsibility for task completion with expected results. Matrix management, in this form, is mandatory, and the project manager must demonstrate the credibility and skills to demand responses. If the respect for this individual does not exist, the process can break down and little will be accomplished.

The project manager is empowered to plan, organize, direct, and control the entire process, much the same as a formal manager is given the authority for a department. However, without the veil of legitimate authority, the project manager must rely on his or her management skills, abilities, respect, and credibility to make decisions and direct the activities. In other words, compliance must be earned on its own merit rather than conveyed on him or her.

♦ *Know when to escalate issues.* One of the key traits needed in a project manager is the ability to be discriminating. As concerns and issues are raised and discussed, the project manager must know, intuitively, when to escalate them to the next or more senior levels. This, of course, will not occur for all issues, but some arise that require top-level decision making or at least top-level awareness.This is the function of the project manager.

Because senior management cannot feasibly be involved with all of the committee's activities and issues, the project manager becomes the liaison and primary interpreter of data to determine its effect or impact on the organization.

♦ *Demonstrate organizational skills.* When a large project is kicked off, there is an intense level of activity that occurs at the onset, and periodically throughout the life of the project. This situation can be compared to spinning plates. Each activity and event is literally a spinning plate. As time progresses, this number grows to the point in which many plates are spinning at the same time. In order to be effective in this process, the project manager must have the organizational skills necessary to manage the activities, simultaneously without losing control. If the project manager is not an organized professional, he or she will have great difficulty managing a large project. This is where project managers often falter. Although most supervisors and managers may be organized in managing projects, the need for organization intensifies beyond the normal level for short-term projects that introduce new systems. The project manager must be aware, in advance, of this intensity and be ready to take on the challenges.

In addition, the project manager should convey a sense of order and control to the project committee. This instills confidence in the process to enable its satisfactory completion. Because committee members will look to the project manager to have an overall grasp of the global aspects of the project, direction, control, and competence will be sought from this individual. Project committee members—especially because of the matrix relationship to the project manager—will demand this type of organization and will be vocal if it doesn't exist.

Facilitation is much more than chairing a meeting. Facilitation is active management—control and coordination of information and issues. When facilitation occurs properly, meetings flow well toward a logical direction, with defined results attained along the way. Facilitation is active and demands energy and focus. When the primary management vehicle of the process is the committee meeting, those skills must be finely honed.

Documentation and Tracking

The final aspect of the project management committee meeting is record keeping. Record keeping for project meetings involves the capture of key information that is raised and discussed in the process. The primary vehicle for this information capture is meeting minutes. Although minutes provide more detailed information than the project plan, they may be too detailed for communication to the CEO and/or senior executives. As a result, a second form of minutes is also needed: the executive summary. Both items are vital to the documentation process and provide the information-capture mechanism needed for management. Both mechanisms are discussed in detail here.

Meeting Minutes. As referred to earlier in the basic format of the project committee meeting, meeting minutes play an important role. Minutes are taken not only for purposes of communication and historical record but also to document specific issues for timely discussion. Because the project plan and Gantt chart are excellent management tools for organizing the project data, communicating its status and monitoring timeframes of the primary segments of the project are addressed. However, for every activity or event, unplanned issues arise. These may be decision points, problems, concerns, or just clarifications. When these concerns surface, if they are not documented and revisited, they may go unresolved. Because the project operates on strict timeframes, the process usually does not stop to catch up. Therefore, the issues raised must be documented in some fashion to refer to it again for follow-up. Because the project plan and Gantt charts are not the appropriate vehicles for this data capture, meeting minutes become the primary mechanism.

Meeting minutes do not have to be formal, nor is it recommended. Parliamentary procedure dictates formalities that should occur with meetings and formal minutes. These rules do not apply to the project process. Minutes should be recorded of the issues. That is, minutes comprise bullets that state the issue raised and its main parts. In addition, if the group decides to take action, that action is also recorded so that it can be reviewed at the next meeting. Bulleted minutes become a form of management tickler, to allow the project manager to revisit the issues and concerns and follow up on their resolution. By capturing those items in the minutes, they can be rediscussed, as needed, at the following project committee meeting.

As indicated in the format of the project committee meeting, one of the four parts of the project committee meeting is a review of the outstanding issues as contained in the meeting minutes. This review should be a reading of the bullets and discussion of its resolution or progress. Ideally, as issues are surfaced, suggested actions will be recommended, and the actions must be assessed at the project meetings to ensure that they do not linger unaddressed.

Meeting minutes, in this way, become an actionable documentation methodology rather than a historical record. Minutes further become an integral part of the meeting for the project manager and committee members alike.

Executive Overview (Minutes). Because the regular meeting minutes are detailed and used as a regular tool for committee meetings, they are generally not appropriate for widespread distribution. Thus only project committee members and the project manager will see them, and another methodology is needed to communicate with the bank CEO and other senior executives.

Summary reporting or creating an executive overview form of the minutes is a process of abridging the minutes to provide, on one page, the highlights or important actions taken by committee members. The executive overview takes its information from the detailed minutes but extracts just that information appropriate for senior management review. In other words, reported major issues and events are what may require senior management involvement or that are necessary for senior managers to see. It is highly recommended to limit these reports to a single page, with one or two lines per bullet.

The executive overview can be prepared as frequently as the project committee meets. However, depending on management's style and wishes, this communication may be less frequent—possibly monthly. In all cases, the report distribution must be regular, once the frequency interval is established. This is important because senior management is seldom involved in the day-to-day project process and therefore, will not be as informed as the project committee and project manager. By providing regular communications to this group, the project manager will keep them informed on major events as well as major issues that require action by upper managers. In this way, they can remain confident of the process direction without having to guess at its progress.

The distribution of executive summaries should be directed to the CEO of the organization as well as executive officers and/or other senior managers who will be affected by the process.

As a final suggestion, senior executives receive a large volume of communications daily. To increase the chances of review of such communications, the one-page document can be produced on an alternative color of paper to catch managers' eyes. This could be yellow, blue or any other eye-catching color that will grab the attention of the senior executive. This is a successful means of communication to this group and will provide confidence in the organization, order, and process of the project.

The key to success in written communications is regularity. Projects are always on demanding time schedules and therefore, any issues that arise must be captured as they occur for prompt review and action. If not, the issues will be missed, with potentially detrimental effects. Proper handling of spur-of-the-moment issues requires a disciplined approach to providing attention to such issues and a sense of urgency for their reporting and resolution.

SUMMARY

Project management is a demanding venture. Once a project is started, it acquires inertia that makes it difficult to alter or stop. As a result, communication becomes not only important but vital to the ultimate success of the project. Chapter 3 focused on the need and importance for good communications throughout the project process. This understanding is important to consider early on in the project life or before it begins, so that all of the important parties to the process are considered. Four primary groups must be considered throughout this process:

♦ Senior management

♦ Project committee members

♦ Users

♦ Customers

Emphasis on these individuals as "parties to the process" was outlined and emphasized. Continual and regular communications to these groups will truly pave the way for much improved understandings and expectations for the changes to take effect. One of the primary vehicles for communication in the project process is the project committee. This is the major forum from which the project is managed by the project manager. The project committee meeting is used as a vehicle for kicking off the process, for all individuals involved at its onset, and for ongoing discussion and review of project progress and issues during the life of the project.

The basic format of the committee meeting consists of a review of the following four items:

1. Review of the project timeline

2. Review of the project plan

3. Review of outstanding issues through the past minutes

4. Discussion of new issues

This standard format must be followed with a high degree of precision, regularity, and order.

The facilitation of the project committee is vested in the project manager. Given a predominantly matrix reporting relationship, with project committee members, the skills required of the project manager must be finely honed to continue this forum effectively. The requirements for sound facilitation are outlined and explained in this chapter. These characteristics are mandatory to ensure that the process is effectively managed.

Finally, documentation of the results of the meeting is of major importance. Documentation is typically accomplished by using meeting minutes. Those minutes consist of two forms: detailed project committee minutes and summarized senior management minutes. In both cases the keys to success are regularity and communication. In addition, the detailed minutes can and should be used as project ticklers for the project manager. In this sense, minutes are an integral part of the process. The development, use, and distribution of these minutes provide the type of communication necessary for the project.

Successful project management will not occur without effective communication. In fact, the need for and purpose of communication are part of the definition of project management. This chapter was devoted to this aspect of project management alone to emphasize its importance and to provide the structure and guidance to ensure that it occurs in a way that will guarantee success.

4

The Bottom Line: Obtaining Results

The beginning of this book referred to concerns about whether the benefits of a project are actually attained as originally anticipated. Whether a project fulfills its mission continues to be an area of skepticism, simply because by the time a project is fully implemented, the commitment and use of resources have been drained. To compound this dilemma, a change generally has occurred. Because of these factors, there is little energy remaining to focus on whether the benefits have truly been achieved in a tangible way. Furthermore, most projects stop at the cutover or implementation of what was set out to be implemented.

   This chapter attempts to provide some guidelines to prevent results from being unmeasurable at the culmination of the project. As the title of this chapter implies, the results and bottom line are at issue. The length of this relatively brief chapter is not a reflection on its importance. For the fact that it merits its own chapter is a statement of the vital nature of measuring results obtained from the project process.

ACHIEVING ORIGINAL PROJECT GOALS

When a project is completed, is there time set aside specifically for an assessment of the original project objectives to results? The answer to this question is typically no. For the reasons previously cited, managers usually devote little energy to do follow-up assessments. So how then do results get measured once they appear to be accomplished, and, is knowing the degree of success important? The first question to be answered is: Is it important to know the specific degree of success?

Without a doubt, accomplishing the original objectives of the project process is vitally important to the organization. When a large project is undertaken, because the justification and approval process commands so much time, energy, and attention to initiate, there is somewhat of a letdown, once the project has been endorsed and has begun. At this point the project analysis is complete and all have essentially agreed to its undertaking. From a decision-making standpoint, however, the real work is just beginning. Closure is not attained until an assessment is made about what was accomplished, whether it made a significant change, achieved the cost saving anticipated, or whether a competitive advantage was garnered.

Therefore, is it important to focus on this? The answer has to be yes because every decision maker who authorized the process has an obligation to the bank and, more importantly, to its shareholders that prudent decisions be made to improve the organization, and that they not be of a frivolous nature. Furthermore, a project is not complete until this aspect of it has been satisfactorily completed.

The previous three chapters have emphasized process, for the most part, during the life of the project. But what happens when the project is actually implemented? Chapter 1 of this book discussed the project's scope, emphasizing the importance of understanding the purpose (mission), outcomes, and benefits to be derived from the project. Because this is an important prerequisite for project initiation, it also should be an important postrequisite analysis after project implementation.

As a starting point for this all-important assessment, the project timeline should contain an event that calls for the review of actual results against the original scope elements. This comparison typically would be the last activity or event to occur in the process. As suggested, the original statement of scope should be analyzed and an assessment be made of each objective and benefit against the reality of its occurrence.

Because many of the objectives and benefits cannot generally be attained immediately, this postproject analysis will not be complete until an adequate period of time has passed. However, the analytical and evaluative process can, and should, nevertheless begin within a short period after cutover. Only when this last phase has been satisfactorily completed can a project truly be considered complete.

The process of analyzing, evaluating, and communicating bottom-line results should be carefully conducted. Once the project implementation is complete and all costs have been incurred, if the objectives cannot be assessed or the benefits cannot be identified as attained, there should be major concern over the efforts conducted thus far. To do a poor job at this point is to invalidate all the work that was previously performed.

The next section outlines the steps and methodologies used to perform such an analysis and finalize the project.

RECAPPING

When the project work has been completed and the project has been implemented or cut over, the analysis phase begins. Part of the reason for this is to tie up loose ends, debrief participants, and ultimately disband the temporary project team. For this reason, the final steps in the project plan should call for a formal "recapping" of the project and ultimate termination of the process. This provides closure to the project and relieves committee members of their temporary responsibilities and allows them to return to the day-to-day work.

The process of recapping involves several parts:

1. Project activity wrap-up

2. Initial review of project scope to results

3. Walkthrough analysis

4. Benefits analysis and recommended actions (process)

5. Tracking mechanisms of benefits

6. Process termination

Each of these steps falls within the final "recapping" stage of the project. The remainder of this chapter is devoted to explaining how each should be used and/or conducted.

Project Activity Wrap-Up

At the time of cutover or implementation, a significant change has usually occurred within the organization. All work previously performed has, for the most part, come to an end. The week of implementation or cutover is spent verifying that the new method or system is performing as it should, identifying bugs or errors, and simply adjusting to the new way. Cutover weeks are always hectic and can be emotion-filled. The individuals involved in the installation at this point are usually engaged in providing help and assistance to users to smooth the transition and resolve any issues that develop as a result of the cutover. This is predominantly reactive and requires the devotion of time and energy until the issues all subside.

If all of the preliminary steps in the project were carried out as prescribed in this book, most of the issues surrounding cutover or implementation will occur only in that first week. A good judge of a project's organization and control is how smoothly and uneventfully the cutover proceeds. Because the cutover week is busy, the first step in "recapping" does not begin until usually a week later. At this time the project manager, with the project committee, begins to identify and evaluate loose ends in order to wrap up the actual project process. This analysis is conducted during a postimplementation project meeting and is a review of the project plan activities for completion.

In addition, an analysis of issues, concerns, and problems is also performed. This initial postimplementation wrap-up meeting will provide a good indication of how much time is needed for wrap-up. If many issues exist, it may be beneficial to continue the wrap-up for the time it takes to clean up all issues and activities remaining on the project plan.

The wrap-up phase should occur only for approximately two to three weeks, if properly managed. Depending on the type of project, such as new software or systems, it is advisable to continue the wrap-up period to extend past a month's end. Month ends are true acid tests for any new system. If problems do not arise at the project cutover, they will most certainly identify themselves at the month end. Once the month end has successfully passed, and all remaining activities and issues are resolved, the wrap-up period is complete.

Initial Review of Project Scope to Results

No project can be considered finished until a review occurs of the original project scope to the project outcome. In other words, did the project do what it originally set out to do? This is the major reason for invoking the project management discipline. For many organizations, the review of scope is often omitted, because it is felt that once cutover occurs there is no need to provide any independent assessment. Unfortunately, omission of this step can negate the positive benefits from using the project management procedures previously outlined.

The performance of this analysis requires little time but can have major benefits to the process. The review should consist of an analysis of the original project scope, as outlined in Chapter 1. The project scope defines the outcomes and objectives of the project. This original scope document should be reviewed against what has actually occurred: Each objective should be compared to the actual achievement. In this way, bank management can gain comfort that the original objectives have been attained. Without this type of analysis, senior management can only guess at whether the project met the planned objectives.

As suggested in this book's Introduction, the scope review is the step most often ignored or missed. If the project is not well organized, when cutover occurs, there will be so much activity occurring that this review becomes seemingly unimportant and burdensome. If not formally planned for in the process it will be omitted. In many cases, the review may seem trivial or anticlimactic, because the implementation of the project may show such obvious changes that this type of analysis may seem unnecessary. Such an assumption couldn't be further from the truth. Every project, regardless of its length or complexity, must have an analysis performed. Only in this way can senior management, and the bank in general, ensure that the project outcome is doing everything that was originally sought at its inception.

The analysis should be originally completed by the project manager and the project committee. Once conducted, a formal writeup and presentation should be prepared and conducted by the project manager to the CEO and senior management of the bank. This is a type of checkpoint meeting that outlines the project results to the original scope. If aspects of the original scope and/or objectives have not been achieved, reasons should be supplied with action plans for their completion, or a statement of its lack of applicability. In this case, subsequent meetings may be required until all applicable objectives are attained.

Walkthrough Analysis

As part of the project closure, it is highly advisable for a physical inspection to occur after the dust has settled. This physical inspection, or "walkthrough," occurs prior to terminating the project process and disbanding the project committee, A physical inspection provides a realistic view of project outcomes.

When practical, the project walkthrough is conducted by the project manager, select project committee members, and available senior management. The primary purpose of the walkthrough is to verify, visually and verbally, whether the system or procedure is working properly. An assessment of operations is an important aspect of the project plan. The people included in the walkthrough process are the user managers and users. The goal is to verify proper functioning from the individuals who are the beneficiaries of the project outcome. The walkthrough will reveal hidden concerns, problems, or changes that are not readily surfaced during project committee meetings or the like.

It is not vital for senior management to be a part of it. Their schedules may not allow for participation. However, this may allow senior management an opportunity to actually see the outcome of the project for which they dedicated the funds.

Walkthroughs do not have to be conducted for every user but rather for a random sampling of users. This selectivity will allow for enough of a test to provide confidence that the system is running with the anticipated results without tying up productive employee time. During the walkthrough it is important to observe how the system operates as well as hear the issues and concerns of the managers and users who work with it. In general, department managers will always be sensitive to changes that occur in their departments. As a result, they will be vocal and a good source of information.

Benefits Analysis and Recommendations

In addition to project objectives contained in the scope, recommendations and benefits also must be considered. To determine the benefits of the project outcome, the assessor should solicit feedback from a number of people. When a project begins there generally is a short list of project benefits anticipated. It is certainly desirable to ensure that these early goals are obtained; however, there are always more. To determine these, opinions should be solicited from department managers and users. Of most importance is soliciting this from department managers. Those individuals who must obtain the benefits, therefore, should participate in the development of these recommendations. Once the managers take ownership for developing recommendations, they will guarantee obtaining them.

Developing recommendations for benefits of the project outcome can be a sensitive process. In some cases, the project outcome may streamline employee duties such that fewer employees are needed to do the job. When this occurs, it is important to get the department managers to accept it; otherwise, they will be unwilling participants to the achievement of the benefits. Where possible, it is advantageous to have the department managers make the recommendations that will achieve the benefits desired. Even though the benefits may be known, to ignore the department managers and users in this process can greatly impede progress toward the achievement of those benefits.

It is important to remember that benefits may not always occur on their own. They must be managed. For this reason, attention should be given to obtaining them in the process of the project itself. Again, as previously stated, this is the step most often over- looked. Because it is seldom built into the project process there is generally little energy left once cutover occurs to pursue these benefits. Such avoidance is not necessarily for lack of desire but rather a need to get back to normal and to the daily routine. If senior management does not emphasize the need to fully obtain such benefits, the project team will disband and everyone will return to business as usual.

This is not to say, however, that there are not benefits that will automatically occur upon implemen- tation. There are. Depending on the type of project, once cutover occurs, this change and all the benefits that go along with it become a reality. Unfortunately, this is seldom the norm because some modification must always occur in order to take advantage of the change. An example of this could be upgrading a system such as a teller system or possibly even a platform automation system. In the latter case, if the system provides for an automatic verification system through enhanced editing parameters, there would be no need for manual verification. Unfortunately, be- cause department managers and supervisors aren't part of the overall process, procedures aren't changed accordingly. When this occurs, users continue to per- form unnecessary duties, and considerable costs are incurred to implement a system that eliminates this need. In short, the benefits must be managed and jobs reengineered to accommodate the changes; otherwise, they will not occur.

Staff members can be habitual in their execution of duties. If change isn't effectively managed, it is difficult to obtain the benefits originally planned for or developed. For these reasons, the benefits analysis phase of the project must be an integral part of the process. Department managers, supervisors, and in some cases users should have input in the process of benefit attainment. When these all occur the project will do what it set out to do.

Tracking Mechanisms of Benefits

Although determining the recommendations necessary to achieve benefits is vital to project success, a management mechanism is necessary to determine whether they have been attained. To some degree, the descriptions used in the project implementation can be used to implement recommendations to achieve the benefits. Once a list of recommendations and their associated bank benefits are determined, the project manager can develop a chart similar to the project plan illustrated in Chapter 2. This form enables the project manager to formally document the recommendation: who will be responsible for obtaining it, the approximate timeframe for its implementation, the status, and finally an estimate of its financial benefit to the bank. An example of this document is shown in Exhibit 4.1.

Exhibit 4.1   Blank Project Benefits Tracking Document

Opportunity/ Benefit Area	Responsible	Begin	End	Actual	Status	Estimated Financial Benefit

The format illustrated is an acceptable form for tracking by the project manager, as well as for presentation to senior management. Of particular note is the column entitled "Estimated Financial Benefit." It is used to estimate the opportunity to the bank in terms of dollar benefits. This column is important because a summation of these opportunities compared with the cost of the project itself will enable financial staff to calculate payback and return on investment. In other words, they will help to determine whether the project was a worthwhile venture to the financial institution.

The project benefits tracking document generally is not as voluminous as the project plan. Most of the recommendations can be documented within one to three pages. Again, the project committee is used as the forum to discuss and monitor the progress of the benefits. The benefits must ultimately be implemented by the department managers and users typically, the functional committee members. If they are not the direct implementers, they would have a reporting relationship with the individual who will implement the opportunity. In either case it is necessary to keep the project committee together to ensure completion of this most important step. The project committee, however, can be scaled back to include only those individuals involved in the actual implementation. The project manager would continue to facilitate the meetings.

Benefit implementation committee meetings should occur on a regular basis—usually every two weeks—until all recommendations have been completed or have been determined as no longer implementable.

Process Termination

The final phase in recapping is to formally terminate the process. This generally occurs when all miscellaneous issues have been resolved, all outstanding project activities are completed, and the benefit recommendations have been attained. At this point, the project manager will solicit feedback from the project committee members and recommend that the process be ended. The formal end of the project halts the convening of regular meetings, minutes, and project updates. The project committee is disbanded and all participants will return to their normal duties.

Before termination is completed, the project manager should circulate a project termination sign-off sheet, as shown in Exhibit 4.2, to the formal committee. The reason for this is to ensure that all committee members have input prior to actually ending the process. Recall from Chapter 1 that the project committee is composed of both functional and control committee members. The control group consists of auditors and other staff functions who will have comments on process termination. By obtaining the signature of these individuals, the project manager documents acknowledgment that the members are satisfied with the implementation and that all outstanding issues have been resolved to their satisfaction.

Once the document is fully signed, it becomes a part of the minutes of the final meeting. In this way

---

Exhibit 4.2   Blank Project Termination Sign-Off Document

PROJECT: PROJECT _____ MANAGER: _____
DATE: _____

    We hereby are satisfied with the implementation of all activities, resolution of outstanding issues, and attainment of benefits pertaining to the above referenced project. Our signatures, provided below, acknowledge this satisfaction, and also concur with the recommendation to terminate the process.

Functional Members   *Control Members*
_____

_____   _____
                                 Audit

_____   _____
                                 Compliance

_____   _____
                                 Purchasing

                                 _____
                                 Systems

                                 _____
                                 Training

                                 _____
                                 Communications

                                 _____
                                 Operations

_____   _____
Project Manager   Date

the working papers are complete with full closure, from process start to finish. At this juncture, the project manager can circulate the final minutes to all committee members, along with the completed/updated Gantt chart and project plan. Now the project manager formally terminates the process. All minutes, project plans, Gantt charts, and other documentation should be compiled into a project folder and archived for future reference and usage.

Recapping is important, if not vital, to the overall success of the project. It should not be taken lightly but should receive as much attention and support as the project process itself. If the steps in the project process are adhered to religiously, recapping will be relatively simple and a process that will be greatly desired. The reason for this is that recapping puts the finishing touches on the project and provides for adequate closure. Just as a graduation ceremony represents the culmination of a long period of study, the recapping stage is the culmination of the work and efforts put forth in the process and should not be omitted.

SUMMARY

Obtaining bottom-line results is the reason or justification for the project undertaking. To omit this most important aspect of the project is to negate the process in its entirety. The purpose of this chapter is to provide structure and organization to this final phase. Structure and organization are necessary because, although vital, reviewing outcomes is the most often overlooked phase of the project. In fact, a review is seldom considered part of the project process, much to the detriment of the work and effort—not to mention the costs—expended to implement the project.

Two major categories are outlined as necessary for this final wrap-up:

♦ Achieving original project goals

♦ Recapping

The achievement of original project goals involves the conscious evaluation of the project outcome to the originally anticipated goals that gave rise to the project. Understanding why this analysis is important and what it reveals will help to not only justify the project but provide comfort that the undertaking did what was anticipated to be done.

Recapping, on the other hand, is another important ingredient. This step provides the necessary procedures for finalizing the project, and taking it to an orderly conclusion. The steps outlined help to organize what should be included in project wrap-up. In most cases, this is the phase most often missing. When projects are implemented or cut over, little energy remains to tie up remaining issues and to guarantee that the benefits, originally set forth, were indeed obtained. To ensure an orderly end and proper closure to the project process, six steps are recommended:

1.   Project activity wrap-up

2.   Review of project scope to results

3. Walkthrough analysis

4. Benefits analysis and recommended actions

5. Tracking mechanisms of benefits

6. Process termination

These steps are designed to finalize all issues pertinent to the implementation process. Moreover, understanding the importance of each factor and why it is needed is critical to the success of the project.. When all is considered, a large amount of time and effort is put into the project's inception, preparation, and process, to minimize the recapping phase is to do an injustice to all prior efforts.

Although each of the steps is important, analyzing and tracking the benefits of the project outcome deserves special attention. Having a good understanding of the relationship between the project itself and the benefits it produces lends perspective to the entire concept. No longer is it simply a project that must be accomplished; it is rather a means toward a specific end. Sometimes this can become obscured, and project committee members and users alike simply go through the motions to complete the project. This isn't necessarily bad, because good executors are always desired in project management. However, by enforcing a "recapping" discipline at the project's conclusion, the project manager grounds the project and adds purpose and meaning to its origin.

As much as it is important to start a project well, it is equally important to end it well. This chapter outlined the elements necessary to give a project proper closure and provided a capstone for ultimate evaluation and assessment. If the project is properly managed, there should be no fear in this approach but rather a welcoming sense of validating the outcome of the project—a necessity for any financial institution given the cost of change.

5

Applications of Project Management in Banking

Throughout this book, most of the discussion has centered around the process of project management. With a firm understanding of this process, virtually anyone can follow the steps necessary to take a project from beginning to end. Because the focus of this publication is banking, the purpose of this chapter is to outline and develop specific uses of this process for a number of banking situations. The following applications are project innovations typical within banks:

♦ Platform automation for personal bankers and commercial sales

♦ Telephone/communication system implementations

♦ Bank mergers

♦ New bank branch acquisitions

This chapter outlines platform automation in detail as a case study identifying the specific project plan activities and explanations necessary for implementation within the financial institution. The specific information is based on actual experiences and attempts to highlight aspects of the projects that will be useful for financial institutions seeking to begin such projects. For each of the remaining applications detailed project plans are provided, in the appendix of this book, for actual usage. Although later applications don't receive the same depth as platform automation, the project plans can literally be copied and used depending on the project the bank is undertaking.

As financial institutions seek to engage in projects involving some of these categories, the actual information can be used directly in setting up the project. Of course, each bank differs somewhat; therefore, individual adaptation will occur in each project plan. However, project managers can adapt these basics to develop the preliminary project scope, in terms of activities. The project plans will assist bank professionals to determine approximate timeframes for project duration.

Coupled with the process and methodologies outlined in this book, the material of this chapter will provide bank management with the tools necessary for successful implementations and ultimate comfort that all aspects are properly addressed and communicated, to ensure maximum efficiency and effectiveness.

PLATFORM AUTOMATION

Automation of a platform is one of the latest major projects in which banks have become engaged over the last few years. Platform automation is the development of a system that provides personal bankers with an automatic means of opening accounts, accessing rates, and various other pertinent pieces of information. The concept behind platform automation is the engineering of the sales process to accomplish three things:

♦ Improve personal banker productivity

♦ Improve sales through greater access to more information

♦ Engineering of the sales process

Because of these objectives, a number of major issues are involved. Among them are:

♦ Purchase or design your own software system

♦ Selection and purchase of software

♦ Selection, purchase, and installation of computer hardware on which to run it

In short, there are many considerations and decisions that must be made from start to finish, to implement a bank's platform automation system. Considering the myriad issues involved, it is imperative to use the project management approach and methodologies espoused in this book. Without this disciplined approach there is considerable risk that the cost of implementation and ultimate timeframes for activation will exceed those projected.

This section provides a template of the activities involved in the process of activating a platform automation system. The events and activities provided are based on actual experience, and are designed to be used in designing and developing project plans and timelines for the bank's own systems.

Project Plan Development

When the bank decides to begin the development of a platform automation system, the project manager must learn what steps and activities are involved, as well as how long the project will take to complete. Before the specific project plan can be developed, it is necessary to develop a basic outline of all phases. There are seven basic phases to the platform automation project process, as follows:

Phase 1: Needs analysis
Phase 2: Development of a concept design
Phase 3: Vendor alternatives and analysis
Phase 4: System design, development, and testing
Phase 5: Hardware/network development
Phase 6: Implementation
Phase 7: Process termination

Each phase requires individual activities and tasks associated with each major category. The expanded outline, indicating the tasks and activities in the order performed, is illustrated in Exhibit 5.1. It is from this outline that the project plan is ultimately developed and Gantt charts are produced. This will be more fully outlined later in this section.

Exhibit 5.1 Expanded Platform Automation Implementation List

1. Needs Analysis
   - Determination of bank areas requiring input
   - Conduct interviews/meetings with bank representatives
   - Summarize needs and findings from interviews
   - Receive flow chart information
   - Develop the statement of scope based on findings
   - Communicate scope and obtain approvals to proceed

2. Development of a Concept Design
   - Select a design team
   - Review scope and flow charts for revisions and changes
   - Develop formal design document structure
   - Develop checklists for vendor evaluation

♦ Disseminate design document and check-lists for review by user management

3. Vendor Alternatives and Analysis
   ♦ Develop a preliminary listing of software vendors
   ♦ Contact the vendors and schedule initial presentations
   ♦ Hold vendor presentations
   ♦ Review and analyze vendor presentation and select final vendors
   ♦ Prepare the request for proposal
   ♦ Submit the RFP to the vendors
   ♦ Schedule and conduct vendor site visits
   ♦ Receive and evaluate vendor proposals
   ♦ Validate responses and review costs
   ♦ Select the vendor
   ♦ Submit for approval
   ♦ Negotiate the contract
   ♦ Execute the contract

4. System Design, Development, and Testing
   ♦ Coordinate the design and development team
   ♦ Develop and customize the application (if required)
   ♦ Develop needed forms
   ♦ Develop the host interface (if applicable)
   ♦ Conduct design team progress check

- Select the pilot implementation site
- Conduct system testing (internal)
- Conduct usability testing
- Incorporate changes and revisions
- Retest the system
- Conduct system stress test

5. Hardware/Network Development
   - Determine the desired system configuration
   - Develop hardware requirement definition
   - Develop hardware vendor lists
   - Develop and submit a request for proposal to the selected hardware vendors
   - Review and evaluate vendor proposals
   - Validate responses and review costs
   - Select the vendor
   - Submit for approval
   - Negotiate the contract
   - Execute the contract

6. Project Implementation

   a. Startup and preparation
   - Hold the kickoff meeting
   - Determine the equipment list
   - Select training specialists
   - Select personnel computer training
   - Select network administrators

♦ Conduct initial review of the training site

♦ Place equipment order

♦ Place training material order

♦ Communication with the host

♦ Develop security (passwords) for users (LAN and mainframe)

♦ Determine the need for forms, and place order

♦ Develop file server staging guide

b. Cabling

♦ Develop cable provider list

♦ Develop a cable standard

♦ Obtain floor plans and locations to be cabled

♦ Develop the request for proposal (RFP)

♦ Submit RFP to cable vendors

♦ Receive and review cable proposals

♦ Validate responses and review costs

♦ Select the cable vendor

♦ Obtain approvals

♦ Place cable order/sign agreement

♦ Install cabling

♦ Conduct postcabling review/signoff and acceptance

c. Communication

♦ Initial bank checkpoint meeting

♦ Equipment installation expectation meeting

- ◆ Bank checkpoint meeting
- ◆ Platform automation expectation meeting
- ◆ Final checkpoint meeting

d. Training

1. Develop training schedules and communications
   - ◆ Network administrators
   - ◆ Personal computer trainer
   - ◆ Training specialists
   - ◆ Back office/support
   - ◆ Executive office
   - ◆ Sales managers
   - ◆ Users
   - ◆ Personal computer skills
   - ◆ Platform system skills
2. Final review and setup of training site
3. Establish and activate training passwords
4. Conduct training
5. Follow-up/refresher training

e. Installation and activation

1. Equipment installation
   - ◆ Physical branch preparation
   - ◆ Staging of equipment
   - ◆ Delivery
   - ◆ Installation
   - ◆ System testing, signoff, and acceptance

2. Platform system activation
   - ♦ Pilot site activation and testing
   - ♦ Branch preparation and setup
   - ♦ Activation of software

7. Process Termination

    a. Postimplementation review

    b. Termination

As shown in Exhibit 5.1, each phase consists of a number of activities and steps that must be conducted. By following the plan outlined, project managers should be able to organize, develop, and implement an effective platform automation system for the bank. In order to provide specific guidelines for this development the rest of this section features step-by-step explanations.

Phase 1: Needs Analysis

The first phase involves the determination of what type of functionality is needed as communicated by the users of the system. Needs analysis is vital for the bank to be successful in developing and/or selecting the type of system that will meet the needs of its users. The tasks involved in this phase are outlined here.

1. *Determine the Bank Areas Requiring Input.* The first activity is to literally select the bank personnel who are involved in the bank's sales management system. This should in-

clude both marketing and sales personnel—
the actual practitioners (that is, personal
bankers). It is important to ensure that a
good mix of users and bank decision makers,
regarding the sales process, are selected for
this activity. The stakeholders in the process
include marketing, personal banker management, personal banker representatives, sales
support (back office) representative, and a
commercial representative.

2. *Conduct Interviews/Meetings with Bank Representatives.* The purpose of this task is to
understand what is needed by the salesforce
to improve and automate the sales process.
The interview should be a structured solici-
tation of information from the participants
based on what is needed in the sales process.
This information will provide the underlying
foundation for the selection and/or development of a tailored system.

In addition, the purpose of the interviews
is to understand how the process currently
flows, in the development of relationships and
sale of bank products to customers.

It is most important to document both
the existing process flow and the needs that
may not be met in a manual system. To
facilitate the meeting, it is prudent to develop
an outline or agenda for discussion. This
document should contain the following information:

1. Current sales process philosophy
2. Current sales process flow
   - Deposits
   - Loans
3. Needed information currently not available or difficult to access
4. Back office/support operational flow
   - Input
   - Handling

3. *Summarize Needs and Findings from Interviews.* Once the interviews are completed, the data should be summarized for ease of access. This document becomes the foundation for system selection and development and should be managed as a key document in the project work papers. Before it is actually completed, a draft of the summary should be reviewed by the interviewees for changes and/or clarifications.

4. *Receive Flow Chart Information.* Part of the purpose of the interview process is to understand the current flow of the sales process. It is desirable to produce a graphical representation of the flow. This visual representation enables the project team and management to easily see and understand how the sales process flows.

5. *Develop the Statement of Scope Based on Findings.* As discussed in Chapter 1, it is

important to define the scope of the project. The reasons for the scope statement are more fully outlined in Chapter 1, but it is predominantly to define the boundaries of the project (where does it start, where does it end, and what is and is not included). At this point, the project manager and team must outline the boundaries based upon the information obtained in all interviews. In other words, does the platform automation system include commercial loans and deposits? Does it include other sales areas such as trust and investments? Finally, how far is the initial development going? No project can be open ended; otherwise, it would not fulfill the definition of a project. Furthermore, time and money will both be limited. The scope of what is to be accomplished must fit the limitations of the resources available.

6.   *Communicate Scope and Obtain Approvals to Proceed.* This step is a sort of checkpoint of the initial project process. Few items have been committed to at this juncture, and virtually no funds have been spent. The summary, process flow (flow chart), and statement scope should be presented to management for adoption, endorsement, and approval to proceed. The goal of this step is to obtain the marching orders. In addition, it is a means of bringing management into the process, thus allowing senior managers to

share in and sign off on the work done prior to proceeding.

Phase 2: Development of a Concept Design

Phase 2 takes the data and background information obtained and translates it into a design and plan for the automated system. This is the actual laboratory work that develops the blueprints to use in the system selection and/or development.

1. *Select a Design Team.* The first, and most important task, is to select the individuals who will actually design the system. The design team is a group of bank employees who actually develop the system blueprints or instructions that will underlie the platform system. The project manager, along with the systems professional responsible for design, must select those who would be a party to the systems design. This is a critical step, because the system must be designed by including the parties who will use it or be responsible for it. If it is not, the system will not be used. For this reason, care must be taken to include professionals who not only are close to the process, but who also have a strong understanding of the bank's sales philosophy. This group usually consists of retail sales managers but should also include at least one hands-on user and a back office operations manager or supervisor.

2. *Review Scope and Flow Charts for Revisions and Changes.* With the design team established, the group must review and become familiarized with the scope statement and flow charts. Before the system blueprint can be "roughed out," the scope and current process must be understood. Any changes required should be made at this juncture.

3. *Develop the Formal Design Document Structure.* Based on the scope and process flow, this step begins the actual design of the structure of the automated system. This is entitled a "concept design" for what the system will do or look like. The design team literally takes the information needs obtained in the needs analysis stage and drafts the plan for the automated system. The draft includes both the flow of the process and the incorporation of those needs identified in the earlier stage.

4. *Develop Checklists for Vendor Evaluation.* From the initial system design, the design team begins to develop checklists of questions and information that must be determined during vendor evaluations. The responses that complete the checklists determine whether the proposed systems provide the desired information or have the capability to be developed. Structured checklists will help the evaluation group to ensure that all areas of information required are addressed.

If structured properly, the checklists will facilitate easy compilation for ultimate evaluation and vendor selection from among the field of vendors.

Checklists should include all critical areas that are part of the concept design. In this way, if some critical feature cannot be met, the vendor may be removed from the list. The construction of the checklist should follow a matrix format that would allow for ease of use and facilitate implementation. An example of a matrix appears in Exhibit 5.2.

The checklist would be used during face-to-face vendor evaluations and/or demonstrations. The system checklist items are determined from the needs analysis sessions and concept design development.

5. *Disseminate Design Document and Checklists for Review by User Management.* The final activity of the concept design phase is to conduct a critical review of the design document. The purpose of this is to communicate back to the individuals who originally provided input to the process—the user managers. This communication strategy provides closure to the needs analysis process and enables the user managers to formally sign off on the concept design prior to committing further time, resources, and money on software products. It is extremely important to obtain this type of review prior to proceeding with the vendor analysis phase.

Exhibit 5.2 Vendor Evaluation Matrix

Vendor Name:			Project Manager:	
Product:			Date:	

System Function/ Capability	Function Available	Function Unavailable	Comments

Phase 3: Vendor Alternatives and Analysis

Phase 3 of the platform automation project involves the determination of vendors, through analysis and selection, for the purchase of the software. If the bank has an information systems department, its staff can assist in this process. Otherwise, it will be completed by the project manager and team.

1. *Develop a Preliminary Listing of Software Vendors.* This rough cut may be the most challenging activity of this phase. Initially a broad listing of platform automation system software vendors should be developed. If the bank has little experience or exposure to software vendors that develop products for this type of function, a good starting place is to consult the American Bankers Association or Bank Administration Institute for suggestions for a preliminary vendor list. These sources should yield leads to a number of vendors.

   The preliminary list should not be massive but should contain enough candidates from which to provide variety and competition. For the purposes of this project, a listing of six to eight vendors would suffice.

2. *Contact the Vendors and Schedule Initial Presentations.* From the rough-cut list, the team contacts vendor representatives to obtain information about the products and support services they offer. This information-gathering

stage can be handled in a number of ways. If the bank has sufficient time, a request for information (RFI) could be developed and mailed. An RFI is a detailed document prepared by the bank project team and sent to the vendors. The RFI contains questions directed at the vendors that are derived from the concept design document and needs analysis. In general, this type of document provides the user with broad information about the vendor: whether the product has the basic capabilities being sought and rough price considerations. The document is used as a means of "weeding out" vendors who cannot meet the needs of the financial institution.

Unfortunately, RFIs take time to prepare, to mail, to receive responses, and finally to analyze them. The RFI approach may not be conducive to the bank's needs. An alternative to the RFI is a vendor demonstration. Vendor demonstrations are opportunities for the vendor to demonstrate the product in a face-to-face meeting.

Based on the listing of vendors developed, contact can be made to arrange demonstrations. The scheduling of vendor presentations should be done as soon as possible. When contact is made with the vendors, general information should be supplied to them about the project and its basic objectives.

In most cases, software vendors are anxious to demonstrate. To that end, it should not be difficult to arrange meeting times. When the coordinator schedules demonstrations, he or she must allot ample time for the demonstration to incorporate time for questions on a casual basis. Generally two or three demonstrations at a maximum could be scheduled in one day. The participants should include the design team (developers) and the project team.

3. *Hold Vendor Presentations.* The presentations are helpful in granting the project team an opportunity to actually see the software in operation. This process is a useful screening device and provides information to the project team that enables a narrowing of the field of players. Prior to the presentations, the basic checklists, previously developed, should be circulated to all participants. This distribution encompasses the design and project teams only. Each participant should have a blank checklist (Exhibit 5.2). For each vendor demonstration, the checklist should be completed and returned to the project manager. Names of the individuals completing the forms should not be required. These evaluations are confidential and should not be shared with the vendors at this point.

4. *Review and Analyze Vendor Presentations and Select Final Vendors.* Upon completion of

all vendor presentations and/or evaluation of
requests for information, the committee tallies and summarizes the results of the vendor
checklists. This summary should be reduced
to a single report indicating a breakdown of
"available" aspects of the system. For the
purposes of narrowing the field, an in-depth
analysis is not necessary. Only an evaluation
of system capabilities among all the proposed
systems is needed. This can easily be accomplished using a summary report that arrays
the results tallied side by side, as in Exhibit
5.3.

This recap of capabilities enables the
project committee to easily assess which systems can provide the most, in terms of the
desired functionality. In addition, the responses on the bottom of the charts indicate
a rough cost. The cost is obtained for com-
parative purposes and is used to evaluate
system capabilities relative to the cost of de-
livering them. During this screening process
it may be found that some vendors are high
in price and may be eliminated. In any event,
costs provide further data for analysis and
narrowing the field.

During this step the project team's goal
is to reduce the field of vendors to two to
three. The surviving vendors are analyzed in
great detail for ultimate selection. When making the selection, the project team should
select vendors who provide the greatest

Exhibit 5.3   Analysis of Preliminary Vendors: Recap Report

Project:				Project Manager:					
				Date:					

System Function/ Capability	Vendor 1	Vendor 1	Vendor 1	Vendor 1	Vendor 1	Vendor 1	Vendor 1	Vendor 1
System Cost								

amount of system capabilities for the price. This should be relatively obvious from the recap report and the demonstrations themselves. The ultimate decision about which vendor to select should be made as a group, based on empirical information and feedback on the demonstrations.

5. *Prepare the Request for Proposal.* The vendors selected must now be fully evaluated for ultimate decision making. This process begins with the development of a Request for Proposal (RFP). The RFP is a document (request) sent to each of the remaining vendors in order to obtain their proposals on their systems. RFPs are standard in the industry; that is, they are used for a variety of reasons and evaluations. In general, the RFP should contain the following:

    1. Overview/introduction of who is requesting the information and for what reason

    2. The scope of what is being asked or will be expected of the vendor

    3. Statement about the timing of return information and who it should be directed to

    4. An overview of how the evaluation will be made

    5. A desired implementation timeframe

    6. Locations at which the system will be used

7. Background information
   - Environment
   - Technical issues/considerations the vendor should be aware of (equipment, operating systems, and so on)
   - Data communications
   - Project process and steps
8. Desired proposal responses

These are detailed issues raised with vendors, among them:

   - Cost/pricing
   - Delivery/installation
   - Training
   - Maintenance
   - On-site support
   - Warranties
   - Reports
   - Upgrades

9. Attachments of pertinent charts or configurations that will prove helpful to the vendors

Requests for proposal are very detailed and provide a wealth of information. The size of the RFP is driven by the complexity of the system needs.

6. *Submit the RFP to the Vendors.* The RFP is mailed to the vendors determined from the evaluation. From the point of mailing ap-

proximately four to five weeks are permitted for return.

7. *Schedule and Conduct Vendor Site Visits.* During the time period awaiting the return of the RFP, vendor site visits should be scheduled. The purpose of these visits is to physically see the software in actual operation, not in a test environment. To schedule visits it is important to obtain a location where the vendor's software is actually in use. This will require the vendor to identify and obtain approvals from an existing client who will permit a demonstration for potential customers. Once this has been determined by the vendor under evaluation, a date can be scheduled to witness the software in operation.

Prior to the site demonstration, checklists, again, should be developed whose answers will form the basis for evaluation. These checklists are essentially the same format as in the preliminary evaluation but will require additional evaluation points. The project committee and design team should re-evaluate the original checklist and develop a listing of other important criteria. It is how well the system meets these criteria that must be considered by the team visiting the sites.

Depending on the location of the site to visit, another consideration is the number of people to schedule to view the product. Demonstration sites are seldom handy to the bank. A select group should be determined who will make the on-site evaluation.

8. *Receive and Evaluate Vendor Proposals.* Vendor proposals require careful attention and analysis. Usually the proposals themselves are voluminous. Once again, the best means of evaluation is a checklist. Checklists enable the evaluators to compare vendors on an "apples to apples" basis to ensure that a consistent and well-thought-out decision is made. During the evaluation process it is important to evaluate each question as it was submitted in the RFP. The responses to these questions will form the foundation for the ultimate decision.

   Each member of the project committee and design team should evaluate each RFP. By doing this, the checklists can be documented for subsequent summarization and decision making. The combination of vendor visits and RFP evaluations will form the basis for the ultimate decision.

9. *Validate Responses and Review Costs.* This step requires an accumulation of all checklists into a summary evaluation document. In order to make a decision, values should be developed for each question from the RFP. Point values should be established on the basis of importance or necessity. In order to do this, several rules should be followed:

♦ Each category, or question on the check-list, should be initially categorized into three broad areas: vital, important, and nice to have. For each of the three categories a maximum point value should be established, as follows:

	Maximum Point Value
Vital	100
Important	50
Nice to have	25

♦ Once each question has been placed in one of the three categories, a total point value for all responses can be established. If the question is answered favorably—that is, it can provide the needed functionality—it should receive most if not all of the points, up to the maximum in the category. As an example, if a question were considered vital and were answered in the affirmative, it should receive from 51 to 100 points. This leaves some opportunity for judgment in terms of the quality of the functionality. Of course, if the software product and/or vendor cannot provide the needed functionality or service, it receives zero points.

By prioritizing and establishing point values based on the relative importance of the questions, the vendors receiving the most points are those who provide the most functionality in the vital areas. In this way, it is the quality of the functionality as opposed to the volume of functions provided that will result in the proper selection.

Finally, once the points are tabulated for each vendor, some form of association to the overall cost of the system is necessary. This association can be in the form of a ratio, number of points per actual dollar expended, or some form of analysis that ties these together. Ultimately, this factor results in an overall ranking of vendors.

10. *Select the Vendor.* Vendor selection is relatively simple once the scoring analysis is completed. As previously discussed, the highest value determined from the validation process indicates the vendor of choice. Once the vendor is identified from the analytical process, the candidate should be discussed by the project committee for consensus.

11. *Submit for Approval.* The proposed vendor, software features, and costs must be approved by the bank in order to proceed. To obtain approval, a standard proposal should be submitted to the bank's steering or executive committee for a signoff to proceed with the purchase or lease. To facilitate approval of the system, the proposal developed outlines the proposed system and purchase or

lease terms. This document should contain the following:

♦ Background/overview: A brief synopsis of the system, its need and planned utilization.

♦ System description: A description of the software, its capabilities, functionality and how it will be used by bank personnel. In addition, the name and location of the vendor.

♦ Cost: The price of the system, including other capital budgeting aids such as: payback period, internal rate of return, ultimate economic life, and amortized costs of the asset.

♦ Benefits/opportunities (justification): The benefits provided that will offset the costs and other opportunities (monetary/non-monetary) that are determined from the system.

♦ Implementation: An approximate time schedule (preliminary) from start to finish. Using this format for approval will streamline the time required and speed the process.

12. *Negotiate the Contract.* Upon receipt of the approval, the project manager (usually) contacts the vendor of choice. The contact with the vendor also is to request the contract or agreement based upon past discussions. The

vendor is informed about being the lead candidate and that upon acceptable agreement to the contract, the vendor will receive the sale.

After receipt of the contract/agreement, the project team should first analyze it to ensure that it contains all of the elements originally desired. This is the business arrangement part of the contract—those aspects that are necessary for day-to-day operation and functionality. Upon satisfaction of this, the agreement should be reviewed by legal counsel to ensure a satisfactory structure for the financial institution.

The last step is to evaluate the pricing structure to determine whether it is acceptable to the bank. Depending on the bank's comfort level, further negotiations may be necessary. It is important to remember that a number of other vendors have been involved in the process. This strengthens the negotiation posture of the bank, because the selected vendor is well aware of the other vendors and is inclined to be flexible in order to retain the bank's business.

13. *Complete the Contract.* The final step is to execute the contract with the vendor. This is completed only after the bank's legal counsel has conducted a satisfactory review and all negotiations have been completed to the bank's satisfaction. Once the contract is signed, a detailed implementation plan is

necessary from the vendor. This will provide the timeframes from which the bank can operate with its own implementation plans.

Phase 4: System Design, Development, and Testing

Phase 4 of the project plan is to design concretely how the system will operate in the actual environment. This may not require actual development, depending on the type of system purchased. In any event testing occurs here as a matter of course. The detailed activities follow.

1. *Coordinate the Design and Development Team.* The design team and the vendor staff meet jointly to develop the necessary plans for implementation. The initial meeting defines the steps and parameters involved, and the choices that must be made to establish the proper parameters of the system.

2. *Develop and Customize the Application (If Required).* At this stage the software purchased may require some form of customization unique to the organization. This is only in the case where the bank purchased software that incorporates customization. In most cases, however, there will be some form of setup that must occur between the vendor and the bank design team. For this reason, time must be devoted to this task, based on the defined nature of the system itself.

3. *Develop Needed Forms.* Platform automation systems usually require alterations to exist-

ing bank forms. Generally, these revisions are discussed with the vendor. Beyond the vendor requirements, however, the project team must involve their current forms vendor and determine lead times and other preparation so forms will be available when needed.

4. *Develop the Host Interface.* The software product selected ultimately must interface to the bank's customer database. If the software is purchased directly from the bank's current service bureau, this does not pose a problem. However, if the bank is an in-house processor or service bureau processor but purchases software from a third party, the interface will be an issue. This activity involves working closely with the bank's mainframe provider and the third-party vendor to work out how the interface will occur. Because of the sensitivity of this issue, it is appropriate to include language in the contract with the vendor that states that the interface can be done and that the vendor has had preliminary discussions with the mainframe provider before the bank signs an agreement. The ability to interface with a mainframe customer database is critical to the entire project. If it cannot be accomplished, it can bring the entire project to a halt.

5. *Conduct Design Team Progress Check.* As the system is being set up, customized, or developed, it is highly advisable to have periodic

design team progress checks. The purpose of such checks is to inform the design team of the actual developmental progress. The primary reason to use them is to ensure that the design team concurs with the setup thus far. If progress checks are not performed, the risk is that the system will be fully developed but will not conform to the needs of the design team. Nonconformity means users are not likely to use the system, wasting the bank's efforts and resources. It is likely that not all design team managers will be involved in development or setup, so they should be informed of periodic progress to remain up to date.

6. *Select the Pilot Implementation Site.* Depending on the size of the financial institution, selecting the pilot site may not be an issue. If the organization has several branches or facilities, a specific location should be targeted for the initial implementation of the system. A pilot site is the first site installed. It is designated as a pilot because the system will be in operation for a period of time before it is implemented at any other site. The pilot site serves as a "live" laboratory to determine how the system operates in an environment like that of the bank. In this way, adjustments or changes can be made before cutover.

It is important to select a representative site that will produce an adequate volume of activity. Otherwise, there may not be enough volume to truly test how all transactions work prior to live implementation.

7. *Conduct System Testing (Internal).* System testing is the activation of the platform system in a test mode in a controlled environment. This is not a live customer contact site but rather a laboratory using test (not live) data.

8. *Conduct Usability Testing.* While the system is still in test mode, users are invited to view it in operation and to actually use it. This involves users physically running the system with test data and test information to simulate how the software might operate in the real world. The users are selected at random. The main purpose of this test is to learn practical issues that could arise from the users' perspective. In this way, many potential problems can be addressed before the system is "brought up" in a live environment.

9. *Incorporate Changes and Revisions.* Based on the information gleaned from both the laboratory system testing and usability tests, changes are made to the system. The revisions can be enhancements as well as corrections of problems noted. The users' feedback offers an opportunity to "fix" the system before it is live.

10. *Retest the System.* Once revisions are made, it is necessary to retest the system in another

laboratory trial. This test is specifically to evaluate the changes and revisions and how they actually worked.

11. *Conduct System Stress Test.* The final test is called a stress test. This, too, is done in the laboratory environment. Similar to the physical stress tests human beings take to check heart strength or endurance, the system stress test checks whether the system can withstand the stress of operation. The purpose is to test the most difficult transactions or to apply pressure to it or, in short, to attempt to overload or overly tax the system to see how it will respond. To complete this test, it is important to note what stresses may occur in the real world. It is valuable to know how this system will react in the laboratory prior to finding out the hard way—during day-to-day operation.

Phase 5: Hardware/Network Development

Obviously, platform systems must run on some type of computer equipment. Platform systems almost always run on personal computer systems in a networked environment. To that end, some of the issues encountered in selecting a software vendor are also encountered in selecting hardware vendors. The following are the activities involved in developing and selecting the hardware and network environment in which the system will run.

1. *Determine the Desired System Configuration.*
    Once the software has been selected, it is
    then necessary to determine on what hard-
    ware the system will run. In most cases,
    banks have a microcomputer environment.
    However, because the microcomputers will
    literally be placed on the desk of each per-
    sonal banker and salesperson, the most cost-
    effective and efficient means of operation is
    through a local area network (LAN). At this
    point, it is vital to know the specifications of
    the software purchased or to be purchased.
    Some software packages may not be issued
    in network versions.

    The next decision point is what type of
    LAN topology should be used. The LAN topol-
    ogy is how the network is connected and how
    information will flow among the microcom-
    puters and the file server. For this decision
    the bank should consult its in-house infor-
    mation systems professionals who serve on
    the project team, its service bureau, or an
    outside systems consultant. Finally, the
    LAN's operating system must be determined.
    Several operating platforms exist in the mar-
    ketplace; however, the bank will likely con-
    sider two: one of Novell's NetWare product
    series or IBM's OS/2. Again, this is a decision
    that absolutely requires systems expertise.
    Furthermore, many software products are
    compatible with one or the other, but not

both. As a result, the selected software vendor and the specifications drive the decision about which operating system to use.

Upon making those decisions the financial institution has the architecture in place for system operation. The remaining tasks in this phase can then be completed. It is important to remember, however, that discussions are necessary with the software vendor to analyze system configuration options. The vendor will likely have support available and can usually provide a wealth of experience in mapping out the system architecture requirements.

2. *Develop Hardware Requirement Definition.* The hardware requirement definition is a determination of the type and amount of hardware, and other peripheral pieces of equipment, including

   ◆ Microcomputers

   ◆ Printers (network and local)

   ◆ Work station operating system

   ◆ Uninterruptible power supplies

   ◆ Tape backup

   ◆ File servers

   ◆ Local area network equipment (control access units, or CAUs, multistation access units or MAUs, lobe attachment modulates, known as LAMs, patch panels, and so on)

The equipment list is based on discussions with the project team of what will be needed at each physical location (if applicable). From this entire list of equipment, the design team tallies quantities for usage in requesting vendor bids. Again, systems professionals will be instrumental in developing the basic hardware requirements.

3. *Develop Hardware Vendor Lists.* Similar to the steps in the software selection, a list of vendors should be created to bid on the equipment lease or purchase. This list should consist of four to five of the major computer hardware manufacturers (IBM, NCR, Hewlett-Packard, Compaq, and so on). From this list, the design team or purchasing department representative on the project committee can make contact with these manufacturers to determine distributors of these products that they would recommend bid. In most cases, each manufacturer's representative will have a good idea about the nearest supplier that can meet the needs of the bank, and will be more than happy to direct the project team to a particular sales office.

4. *Develop and Submit a Request for Proposal to the Selected Hardware Vendors.* As with the software selection, a request for proposal

(RFP) is needed to provide information to the potential vendors to give them an opportunity to propose on the equipment definition required. The development of the RFP should follow the same structure as outlined previously in phase 3, task 5. One of the main parts of the RFP, however, is a complete list of the equipment and quantities needed. This is vital in order for them to properly bid on the system.

Once the RFP is developed it should be sent directly to each vendor for response. Approximately four to five weeks should be permitted for response.

During this period in which the bank is awaiting responses to the RFPs, the project team may request from each vendor that a test system be set up at the development site. The purpose of this is to gain familiarity with the various systems and have an opportunity to get a sense of the various systems ergonomically. Most vendors will be more than happy to do this for a period of a few weeks to aid in the decision process. It is also desirable to invite several future users of the system to use the test systems to see what they like and don't like. This not only involves them in the process but also provides valuable information to the project team for assistance in decision making.

5. *Review and Evaluate Vendor Proposals.* The proposals received from the vendors should

be tabulated and compared with one another for decision-making purposes. Unlike the software analysis, evaluation of hardware is straight forward: Most of the vendors involved have proven reputations in terms of system reliability the deciding factors will rest with

♦ Cost

♦ Support

♦ Maintenance

♦ Installation/setup support

♦ Project management assistance

In these five areas, the ultimate determination will be made. To facilitate this decision process, the five factors can be ranked in priority order with maximum point values assigned. Based on experience, the ranking can generally be arranged as follows:

1. Cost

2. Maintenance

3. Support

4. Installation/setup support

5. Project management assistance

6. *Validate Responses and Review Costs.* Point values can be assigned as suggested in the software analysis by establishing, priorities as follows:

	Maximum
Cost	200
Maintenance	150
Support	100
Installation	75
Project Management	50

Each category can be evaluated for each vendor response. The point value assigned would be a value within the range, up to the maximum for each category. For example, if vendor A's support is deemed very good but not the best, the vendor could receive a point value of 76 out of a possible 100 points for that category. The quality of the response dictates the subjective assignment of points, per category.

Once this validation has been completed for each vendor, a comparison can be made. The comparison of point values is what provides direction toward selecting the vendor of choice. In virtually all cases, costs and maintenance play a major role in the actual selection. Although support, installation assistance, and project management are important, these may be areas the bank can provide internally.

7. *Select the Vendor.* Before the vendor is selected for approval, a member of the team should contact all of the customer references provided in the vendor proposal. This is of

major importance to the ultimate decision because it will provide a means of understanding whether the vendor actually can provide what it says it can. Questions of the references should focus on four of the priority areas:

♦ Quality and responsiveness of maintenance support

♦ Quality, responsiveness, and availability of telephone support

♦ Capability qualifications and quality of installations, as well as timely completions

♦ Capability and quality of project management

References are important to the selection process, because customers' testimonials will shed light on how seriously the supplier focuses on long-term relationships.

8. *Submit for Approval.* Once the vendor has been determined, it is necessary to obtain senior management approval to proceed with the vendor. As with the software approval, a proposal document should be submitted to the bank's senior management for ultimate signoff.

9. *Negotiate the Contract.* The vendor who has been selected should provide a written agreement that provides the legal structure for the

future purchase relationship. Negotiating the agreement should focus on obtaining an acceptable purchase price given the volume of equipment required. As with software, additional incentive is provided by the fact that there are several vendors to turn to if necessary. This will always strengthen the negotiating position.

10. *Execute the Contract.* Finally, the contract is signed and submitted to the vendor. This triggers the activities that will occur over the next several weeks and/or months during project implementation.

Phase 6: Project Implementation

Phase 6 comprises a major thrust of the entire project. Implementation brings everything together and concentrates on moving the project from "concept to reality." Project implementation involves five subphases, as follows:

♦ Startup and preparation

♦ Cabling

♦ Communication

♦ Training

♦ Installation and activation

A. *Startup and Preparation.* Twelve steps are involved in the startup and preparation phase, as follows:

1. *Hold the kickoff meeting*—The kickoff meeting is used once again to set the tone and outline the actual steps involved in implementation. The attendees at the kickoff meeting comprise the project team and other appropriate users as may be involved occasionally. The group should conform to the structure outlined earlier for the kickoff meeting. This meeting summarizes what has occurred thus far and what is about to occur during implementation.

2. *Determine the equipment list*—The equipment list is determined based on the needs of the specific location to be implemented.

   Such a list should be detailed, including hardware specifications, quantities, and prices. The list simulates that of an order form. When completing the list, it is important that it be reviewed by the branch or department manager to ensure that all data is included. Equipment lists should include all system hardware, printers, local and network equipment, and software.

3. *Select training specialists*—Training specialists are personal bankers or other appropriate bank salespeople who have been instructed on the platform automation system. The reason they are selected to be instructed and in turn to teach other users is to provide additional sources of on-site assis-

tance for users once they have been trained and the systems have been activated. These individuals can be available on site when the salespeople review their training. In this way they can provide immediate support for questions or general system usage assistance when users need it most: immediately following training. Training specialists are generally needed at the site for approximately one week. This usually provides ample time to allow users to become comfortable with the system, with support close by.

4. *Select personal computer trainer*—A personal computer trainer is needed to provide basic microcomputer hardware and software training. This type of training can be accomplished in many ways—via videotape or certainly stand-up classroom lecture. Whatever the medium and format, an individual is needed to coordinate computer training and/or actually instruct the users.

    When users move to a networked PC environment, it should not be assumed that everyone knows how to operate a microcomputer. The four areas where training typically is needed are

◆ Microcomputer basics
◆ Local area network basics
◆ Operating system usage
◆ Other application software usage

Microcomputer basics deal with the operation of a PC (turning it on and off, using the keyboard, printing, and so on). LAN basics instruct users on the various shared drives, getting access to the network, and so forth. The last two areas focus on software. At least some rudimentary understanding of the operating system is helpful.

The microcomputer trainer could be the bank's existing trainer, an outside resource, or a computer-literate employee. In any event, this training is vital.

5. *Select network administrators*—In multiple- or single-site organizations there is always a need for one or several network administrators. These are not full-time positions but rather designated individuals who are responsible for "level-one" technical support at the site. Support would include basic troubleshooting of the file server, basic hardware operation, and acting as liaison to more detailed support. Because the file server functions as a sort of "mini-mainframe," someone locally must be responsible for its care and basic operation. In addition, file servers and LANs have other peripheral equipment that may require additional work for updating and day-to-day work.

    Network administrators are a must for any site having a LAN.

6. *Hold initial review of the training site*—Before the trainer conducts either microcomputer or the platform system training, a training site must be selected and developed. The training site should be networked and have approximately four to six microcomputers and printers. A television and VCR are also required for video-based training. Because users must be educated on microcomputer usage as well as the platform software, a considerable amount of time will be spent in the room. For this reason, it should be reviewed, evaluated, and finally set up for training. Upon completion of all training, the equipment in the room can remain or it can be deployed for productive usage elsewhere.

7. *Place equipment order*—From the detailed hardware list, an order can then be placed to the hardware vendor previously selected. This should be a written detailed order, including agreed-on pricing, and quantities. This is important documentation and can be used to verify invoices against what was ordered. Orders should always be placed six to eight weeks in advance of installation deadlines.

8. *Place training material order*—Training materials, such as workbooks, videotapes, and slides, must be ordered. The order should be

placed at the same time as the equipment order to ensure a timely delivery.

9. *Communicate with the host*—Depending on the bank's mainframe processing arrangement, communication is necessary with this group. The reason is that the platform system will communicate and retrieve information directly from the host. As such, it is necessary to determine what requirements are needed to enable the local area network to communicate directly to the host as another device on the overall network. The mainframe organization is likely to have a schedule when this can be done, and will need specific information in the form of physical units (PUs) in order to handle this request. Without this necessary step, the system would not be established as a device for communication to the host.

10. *Develop security (passwords) for users (LAN and mainframe)*—Because the architecture developed involves a local area network, access security to data files must be established. Security features include user IDs that are created at the file server. This will allow anyone using the proper ID to log on to the local area network. These IDs and users must be assigned and be ready for input to the server prior to its installation. Initially this will be accomplished at staging.

In the future, however, the network administration can add or delete user IDs.

The platform automation system will have a separate password. The reason is that it will pull information from the main database and perform file maintenance to the system directly online. In this way, a user ID similar to typical mainframe access must also be assigned to any user of the platform system. The ID can be assigned directly by the bank's security manager but must also be communicated to the LAN administrators and information systems or project team for staging purposes.

11. *Determine the need for forms and place order*—From an earlier design step that identified forms, the quantities needed should be calculated and ordered. Again, the order's delivery date should correspond with the activation date of the platform system. Ample time should be allotted for receipt of forms, because system activation will be delayed if the forms are not available when needed.

12. *Develop file server staging guide*—The last preparation step is highly technical. It should be accomplished by the hardware vendors in conjunction with the bank's internal microcomputer specialist and/or an outside consultant. This guide sets the parameters and procedures for loading software, configuring

the system, testing and shake out, and ultimate acceptance of the LAN itself.

The staging document should be a "hard copy" document outlining how the server is configured and the steps involved. It will be instrumental for adding future servers and networks to the group.

B. *Cabling.* Twelve steps are required for proper cabling and interfacing of the LAN:

1. *Develop cable provider list*—Lengths of cabling among network components are required on the system site. Cabling involves pulling wires through floors, ceilings, and walls, terminating at a box on the floor or wall. It is to this box that the microcomputer adapter card cable will be plugged, thereby activating it on the network.

    Many cable suppliers and variations exist in the marketplace. Regardless of the number of sites involved, it is always desirable to develop a list of potential cablers from whom a bid will be requested. In this way, the bank will be assured of a good price.

    A useful list of potential vendors relies on the experience of those suggesting vendors. There are many good cablers in the market—and many bad ones. The list should be developed based on some experience. The low-cost bidder is not necessarily the best. An outside telecommunications consultant can help the bank to make a wise choice, as

can other systems professionals who have
had network background. The list should include five to six cable vendors.

2. *Develop a cable standard*—Before installers
    can begin cabling, it is necessary to write a
    cable standard for the type of wire, jacks,
    outlets, and other elements of the LAN. The
    cable standard must be done to ensure com-
    munality of cabling for all current and future
    sites. Only in this way can the bank guaran-
    tee absolute compatibility.

    Cable standards are complex and typi-
    cally require several pages to describe. The
    development of this document must be ac-
    complished either by or with the assistance
    of an outside telecommunications consulting
    firm. This should be developed in conjunction
    with the bank's telephone system and plans
    as well as with the needs of the specific local
    area network. To that end the hardware
    provider should also be involved to provide
    assistance to the telecommunications con-
    sultant.

    Once the standard is developed, it can
    be reused for new sites. It can literally be
    completed and then handed to any cable ven-
    dor to give the needed direction for implemen-
    tation.

3. *Obtain floor plans and locations to be cabled*—
    Before taking further steps, each location,
    requiring cabling, must be drawn out in the

form of "rough" floorplan. This does not have to be an architectural blueprint but rather a "hand-drawn" document to a reasonable scale. The "hand-drawn" floorplan should show desks and work spaces where micro-computers and/or printers will be located. This should be in the form of a symbol that indicates the desired equipment. In many cases a "cable pull" to a desk will indicate the need for a computer, but also the need will exist for a phone. When cabling is conducted both voice and data cabling can/and should be done simultaneously. This saves both time and money. In this sense, the floor plan should indicate which locations require "voice only," "data only," or "voice and data." These can be illustrated by symbols, with an appropriate legend explaining their meaning.

4. *Develop the request for proposal (RFP)*—An RFP should be developed to be sent to each cable vendor on the list. Again, this can conform to the format of the hardware and/or software RFPs previously discussed. The RFP should include at least a copy of the cable standard and floor plans of all sites to be cabled. Outside assistance is desirable for the preparation of this document; telecommunications professionals provide the most expertise.

5. *Submit the RFP to Cable Vendors*—The RFP should be mailed to each cable vendor, al-

lowing approximately four weeks for return. Aside from the cable standard itself, the RFP for cablers is less detailed and therefore can be completed relatively quickly.

6.   *Receive and review cable proposals*—The returned proposals should be reviewed by the project manager, outside consultants, and appropriate staff. A cost-comparison matrix can be developed, arraying pricing by vendor to direct the team to the top candidate. In most cases cost and timing of completion will be the primary selection criteria. Quality, too, is important, but this must be determined through reference checks.

7.   *Validate responses and review costs*—With the proposal data recapped, the project team may wish to point-score the various questions as outlined previously for software evaluation. This is a more objective means of evaluating cable vendors.

8.   *Select the cable vendor*—Selection of the cable vendor can be made once the data is tabulated and a reference check is made. Each cable vendor should provide a number of references as part of the RFP. It is vital to check the references and base an assessment on the quality of work the references state was performed. Never assume that, since the list was recommended by a telecommunication professional, all are of equal quality. Poor quality cabling will result in poor service or

a lack of functionality, which the bank could pay for during the years to come.

Upon satisfactory reference checking and analysis, the top vendor should be designated as the vendor of choice.

9. *Obtain approvals*—Because of the cost involved, proposals should be submitted to the bank's executive or management committee for approval. A proposal document should be prepared, as previously outlined.

10. *Place cable order/sign agreement*—Upon approval of the proposal, contact should be made with the cable vendor requesting a formal agreement to proceed. The agreement should specify the agreed-upon pricing, as well as the specific timeframes in which the cable installation will start and end. It is highly desirable to include clauses that stipulate a penalty for late starts and/or finish dates.

11. *Install cabling*—The vendor will begin cabling per the agreed schedule. Typically installation occurs during working hours, so the branch management should be informed in advance and advised that some disruption will occur at the site. During cabling the project manager should verify that the installers began on schedule and should contact them halfway through for a progress check.

12. *Postcabling review/signoff and acceptance*—
    The final step in cabling is a physical walk-
    through. The project manager should walk
    through the site, with floorplan in hand, with
    the cable foreman to verify each site. This
    sight verification should consider whether

    ♦ All locations are clearly labeled
    ♦ All cable locations are properly terminated
    ♦ The work area has been cleaned up
    ♦ All work should conform to the detailed
      cable standard. Signoff should not occur
      until the quality of cabling has actually
      been verified.

C. *Communication.* Five meetings are held to manage dissemination of information:

1. *Initial bank checkpoint meeting*—Checkpoint
   meetings are a means of keeping the bank or
   locations management informed of the project process. Most of the work on the project
   is carried out with the project team, which
   typically does not include other bank senior
   management. This first meeting appraises
   managers of what is about to occur at their
   branches and to ascertain their feedback,
   concerns, or questions. It is a means of making the project manager available so bank
   managers have an opportunity to comment
   on what is going on. This meeting should

consist of the CEO and other senior managers—typically the management or executive committee.

2. *Equipment installation expectation meeting*— Unlike the checkpoint meeting, the second meeting is an informative session. It should be scheduled approximately one to two weeks prior to equipment installation and delivery. Its purpose is to inform the bank's managers of what to expect from hardware delivery, installation, and training. The session should include all bank managers whose staffs will be affected by the installation and other bank managers who should be made aware of its occurrences. This tends to keep managers proactively informed so that they can, in turn, answer questions and concerns from their employees as they arise. This open communication aids in keeping bank managers part of the process.

3. *Bank checkpoint meeting*—This is a midpoint checkpoint meeting conducted for the same group that attended the initial checkpoint meeting. The follow-up aids both senior management and project team alike in hearing the concerns of this group, and obtaining candid feedback. Because this is organized, it provides an outlet for senior management to use as progress is made.

4. *Platform automation expectation meeting*—
    Similar to the hardware expectation meeting,
    this session is conducted approximately one
    to two weeks prior to the activation of the
    first platform automation site. Again, the
    same group of managers is involved and the
    session is established as an informative
    meeting. This educates managers on the
    training commitments required of his or her
    staff as well as what will happen and when.
    Proactive information sessions of this sort
    will diffuse as well as educate.

5. *Final checkpoint meeting*—The final check-
    point meeting should be scheduled when all
    training, installation, and system activation
    has occurred at all sites. When this is com-
    pleted, the bank's senior management and
    CEO should have an opportunity to recap
    their concerns, comment on the process, and
    voice any problem areas detected during the
    process. This capstone meeting provides clo-
    sure to the process and provides senior man-
    agement with a forum for comments.

    Typically, the final checkpoint meeting
    is the last formal meeting held with bank
    senior management.

D. *Training.* Five phases of training should occur:

1. *Develop Training Schedules and Communica-
    tions*—Training schedules must be developed
    and communicated in advance to ensure that

all pertinent parties can participate. This step should not be taken lightly; it is important for the overall success of the project. Training schedules must first be communicated to user management to ensure that there are no hidden conflicts that the group is unaware of. Furthermore, by communicating first with user managers, they will be certain to ensure that their staff members attend the training. Training schedules must be developed for

◆ Network administrators (1 day)
◆ Personal computer trainer (1/2 day)
◆ Training specialists (4 to 5 days)
◆ Back office/support (1/2 day)
◆ Executive officers (1/2 day)
◆ Sales managers (1/2 to 1 day)
◆ Users:
   ◆ Personal computer skills (1 day)
   ◆ Platform system skills (4 to 5 days)

2. *Final review and setup of training site*—A final walkthrough or review of the actual training lab is necessary as a means to ensure that all equipment is in working order and ready to go. The short time this requires is well worth the effort because once resources are scheduled and users are attending the session, it is very difficult to reschedule them if something doesn't work. Furthermore, be-

cause each session will likely be scheduled back-to-back, it could be disruptive to move a mass of people around.

3. *Establish and activate training passwords*— For both the LAN and the platform system, it is necessary to have passwords set up for usage on the test system in the training room. Those passwords enable trainees to access the test system to undergo hands-on training in a simulated environment. Again, it is advisable to check, in advance, whether passwords have been assigned and are workable, in advance of conducting your first training session.

4. *Conduct Training*—Once schedules are developed, training can commence. Actual training will require time on the part of the bank employees; therefore, it is important that employees and their managers understand that work disruption is inevitable before employees begin their sessions. Furthermore, training must be mandatory; it is not optional. It must be emphasized that with a platform automation program, once the system is activated, there is no return to the manual system. In that sense, it is vital that the parties commit to training and make a serious effort to complete it.

Once training has occurred it is important that the user return immediately to the platform and begin using either the microcomputer, or platform system. Immediate and continued practice will speed the education process.

5. *Follow-up/refresher training*—Finally, after the platform system has been in operation for at least four to six weeks, additional training is needed. The additional training is described as "refresher training" in that its purpose is to review the original training that was conducted, resolve difficulties, answer questions, and review more advanced topics. After four to six weeks of actual system usage, users will have well-formed questions in which to ask and have much greater familiarity in general with the system.

E. *Installation and Activation.* Two major actions compose the installation and activation stage:

1. Equipment installation—One of the final steps of the implementation phase is the actual installation of the equipment hardware and software. This activity is further broken down into a number of subtasks that actually complete the system installation. The subtasks are

   ♦ *Physical branch preparation:* Prior to actual installation of computers and peripherals, it is necessary to prepare the physical site to accommodate them. Preparation involves reviewing requirements for power, lighting, and communications. In addition, each desk should be analyzed to determine how cables are routed to where the computer will be. In some cases it will be necessary to cut grommets in the desks to route cables, for safety and appearance. Desks should be cleared to accommodate the microcomputer and work space for documents. Space should be available for local printers, if any.

In short, room must be made for the physical equipment. This should occur a minimum of two weeks prior to actual installation.

♦ *Staging of equipment:* Equipment staging is off site and occurs the week prior to installation. This typically is accomplished by the equipment vendor and involves loading software, setup, testing, and acceptance of the system in a test environment. The guidelines for this are contained in the staging document, previously developed.

♦ *Delivery:* The delivery of the equipment should be targeted to occur one to two days in advance of planned installation. On receipt of the hardware, the network administrator should verify receipt of goods to the actual purchase document.

♦ *Installation:* Installation involves the physical setup of microcomputers, printers, LAN equipment, and other peripherals. Ideally, this installation should occur after-hours or during the weekend. Installation would be conducted by the hardware vendor, contract personnel, or internal staff if they are qualified.

♦ *System testing, signoff, and acceptance*: After the system has been installed, each workstation should be physically tested executing a defined list of functions and commands. An acceptance document checklist should be developed and used for the signoff. The hardware vendor and/or the installer can develop this document. Each item on the list must be checked off before the entire system can be termed "approved."

2. *Platform system activation*—The final task is the activation of the platform at the physical site. Activation generally occurs approximately three to four weeks after hardware installation. This allows ample time for the user to practice microcomputer usage before being trained on the platform software. Three subtasks are involved in this section:

♦ *Pilot Site Activation and Testing:* Immediately after the physical equipment is installed, the platform system should be activated at one workstation to test how it works. This is conducted prior to formal platform training. Testing should involve actual ability to access the system but also to print reports and documents. This testing should occur approximately four to five weeks in advance of system activation.

♦ *Branch Preparation and Setup:* Similar to preparation of the physical site for the equipment, additional preparation is required in advance of system activation. Approximately one week prior to system activation—actually while the salesperson is in platform training—the platform desk must be prepared for the change. This preparation involves supplying workstations with the necessary forms that will be used. Remember, once the user returns from training he or she will be working with an automation system and not the manual one. In order to make this transition, the users' workstations must be physically set up to make an immediate change.

♦ *Activation of Software:* Finally, when the user returns from intensive platform training, the platform software should be operable. This activation can be accomplished by the network administrator. Therefore, workstations for users in training should be activated while they are away, so that when they return to their desks they begin using the new platform system.

Phase 7: Process Termination

Process termination is the last identified task of the project. It is formally outlined in order to have a demarcation point when the project process has formally ended. Two categories of activities are involved in this phase:

♦ Postimplementation review

♦ Termination

1. *Postimplementation Review.* The postimplementation review involves a final walkthrough or assessment of project tasks to determine whether any remain open or uncompleted. The purpose of the final review is to tie up loose ends, determine which tasks still remain unfinished, and decide how to complete them. This review is important to ensure that the project does not end with important tasks left undone. In general, this step should be conducted approximately the week following final cutover or installation (at the final site).

2. *Termination.* Final termination is a formal end to the project and its process. Termination cannot occur until all loose ends and open issues are resolved. Project meetings should continue until open issues are resolved. When the wrapup occurs and the project plan is virtually complete, the project manager should terminate the project. Termination includes a final project committee

meeting at which the team gives a final signoff on a document that indicates that all aspects have been completed to the satisfaction of each committee member. This document then becomes part of the working papers of the project for practical purposes.

It is recommended that the final project committee meeting occur after a month-end has occurred. The reason is that month-ends tend to be sensitive times. If something is likely to go awry it will do so at a month-end. Scheduling the final meeting approximately one to two weeks after the month-end will be sufficient to identify any issues requiring resolution.

Finally, after project termination a communication should be published to bank management that the project has formally ended.

The Appendix of this book provides a detailed project plan template that can be used as a shell for readers' projects. By following the basic project plan template, any bank should be able to implement a platform automation system successfully.

TELEPHONE/COMMUNICATION SYSTEM IMPLEMENTATION

Many financial institutions have begun or have completed an upgrade to their existing telephone system. The primary purpose for this is to take advantage of the advent of voice mail and digital telephone systems. Furthermore, the world of telecommunications is moving toward integrating voice and data communications on the same circuits. This has implications not only for telephone communications but for all data communication needs. Such an innovation would involve branch-to-branch microcomputer connectivity for the development of wide area networks, digital private branch exchanges, and other such technical information-sharing approaches.

Telephones and communication networks (voice and data) require detailed activities to ultimately implement an integrated system. To facilitate the implementation of projects of this nature, a detailed project plan template is contained in the appendix of this book. The template can be used to develop and implement a communications system project by using the detailed tasks as developed. Many of the tasks may be similar to those found under platform automation and, as a result, can be reviewed for further understanding.

MERGERS AND ACQUISITIONS

Many financial institutions are in the midst of either acquiring new organizations or merging existing separately chartered banks. The issues involved in affecting a merger and/or consolidation can be reduced to a number of key project activities. These project activities allow for an organized, timely, and well-structured plan, which ensures a smooth technical and/or physical transition. Detailed project plans are provided in the appendix that can be used by the reader to guide most merger and acquisition processes.

SUMMARY

The purpose for this chapter has been to provide actual working examples of project plan events and activities for immediate usage. In many cases, once a major project is undertaken the greatest difficulty is getting it started, organizing it, and identifying all tasks and activities that are required. Within this chapter, detailed project plans and activities are provided for some of the primary types of bank projects. The detailed project plans contained in the appendix are designed for immediate usage.

Finally, platform automation is a timely topic in banking. Understanding and identifying the activities involved can spell the difference between success and failure. For this reason the tasks outlined have been based on successful applications in a banking situation, and are explained to enable bank employees to develop and manage their own projects' processes.

Appendix I

Platform Automation Project Plan Template

Platform Automation Project Plan Template

Project:	Platform Automation System	Project Manager:					
Page:	1	Date Updated:					

Event/Activity	Responsible	Weeks Precutover	Target Begin	Target End	Actual End	Status
A. NEEDS ANALYSIS						
1. Determine bank areas requiring input	Project Team	78				
2. Conduct interviews/meetings with bank representatives	Project Team	76				
3. Summarize needs/findings from interviews	Project Team	73				
4. Receive flow chart information	Project Team	70				
5. Develop statement of scope based upon findings	Project Team	68				
B. DEVELOPMENT OF A CONCEPT DESIGN						
1. Select a design team	Project Team	65				
2. Review scope and flow charts for revisions/changes	Design/Project Team	65				
3. Develop formal design document structure	Design Team	63				
4. Develop checklists for vendor evaluation	Design Team	58				
5. Communicate design document and checklists for review by user management	Design Team	56				
C. VENDOR ALTERNATIVES AND ANALYSIS						
1. Develop preliminary list of software vendors	Project Team	56				
2. Contact vendors and schedule initial vendor presentations	Project Team	54				
3. Vendor presentations	Project/Design Team	52				
4. Review/analyze vendor presentations and select final vendors	Project Team	49				
5. Prepare request for proposal	Project Team	48				

272

Platform Automation Project Plan Template (continued)

Project:	Platform Automation System	Project Manager:				
Page:	2	Date Updated:				

Event/Activity	Responsible	Weeks Precutover	Target Begin	Target End	Actual End	Status
6. Submit RFP to vendors	Project Team	46				
7. Schedule and conduct vendor site visits/review checklists	Design/Project Team	44				
8. Receive and evaluate vendor proposals	Design/Project Team	40				
9. Validate responses and review costs	Design/Project Team	39				
10. Select vendor	Design/Project Team	37				
11. Submit for approval	Project Team	37				
12. Contract negotiations	Project Team	35				
13. Contract execution	Management	30				
D. SYSTEM DESIGN, DEVELOPMENT AND TESTING						
1. Cordinated the design team	Project Team	30				
2. Develop/customize application (as required)	Design Team	30				
3. Develop forms	Design Team	30				
4. Develop host interface	Design Team	30				
5. Design team progress check	Project Team	20				
6. Select pilot implementation site	Design/Project, Mgmt	18				
7. Test system internally	Design Team	15				
8. Test user usability	Design Team/Users	10				
9. Make changes and revisions	Design Team	8				
10. Retest system internally	Design Team	5				
11. Perform system stress test	Design Team	3				
E. HARDWARE/NETWORK DEVELOPMENT						
1. Determine desired system configuration for handling	Project Team	25				
2. Develop hardware requirements definition	Project Team	25				
3. Develop hardware vendor lists	Project Team	24				

273

Platform Automation Project Plan Template (continued)

Project:	Platform Automation System	Project Manager:				
Page:	3	Date Updated:				
Event/Activity	**Responsible**	**Weeks Precutover**	**Target Begin**	**Target End**	**Actual End**	**Status**
4. Develop and submit request for proposal to vendors	Project Team	23				
5. Review/evaluate vendor proposals	Project Team	19				
6. Validate responses and review costs	Project Team	19				
7. Select vendors	Project Team	17				
8. Submit for approval	Project Team	16				
9. Negotiate contract	Project Manager	15				
10. Execute contract	Management	13				
F. IMPLEMENTATION						
1. Start-up/preparation:						
-Kickoff meeting	Project Team/Users	25				
-Determine equipment list	Project Team	10				
-Select training specialists	Project Team/Users	12				
-Select microcomputer trainer	Project Team/Users	6				
-Select network administrators	Project Team/Users	6				
-Hold initial review of training site	Project Team	6				
-Place equipment order	Project Team	8				
-Place training material order	Project Team	6				
-Communicate with host	Project Team/I.S.	6				
-Develop/assign user IDs	Project Team/Users	15				
-Determine forms needs and place order	Project Team	8				
-Develop file server staging guide	Project Team	10				
		12				
2. Cabling:						
-Develop cable provider list	Project Team	22				
-Obtain floor plans and locations to be cabled	Project Team/Users	20				
-Develop cable standard	Project Team/ Consultants	21				

Platform Automation Project Plan Template (continued)

Project:	Platform Automation System	Project Manager:				
Page:	4	Date Updated:				

Event/Activity	Responsible	Weeks Precursor	Target Begin	Target End	Actual End	Status
-Develop request for proposal	Project Team	17				
-Submit request for proposal	Project Team	15				
-Receive/review cable proposal	Project Team	10				
-Validate responses and review costs	Project Team	10				
-Select cable vendor	Project Team	8				
-Obtain approvals	Project Team/Mgmt	6				
-Place cable order/sign agreements	Project Team	5				
-Conduct cabling	Cable Vendor	3				
-Have postcable review/signoff and acceptance	Project Team	1				
3. Communication:						
-Hold initial bank checkpoint meeting	Project Mgr/Sr. Mgmt	2				
-Install equipment expectation meeting	Project Mgr/User Mgmt	1				
-Hold bank checkpoint meeting	Project Mgr/Sr. Mgmt	-4				
-Platform automation software activation expectation meeting	Project Mgr/User Mgmt					
-Hold final checkpoint meeting	Project Mgr/Sr. Mgmt	-8				
4. Training:						
-Develop training schedules and communications for:	Project Team/Users	7				
-Network administration		7				
-PC trainer		7				
-Training specialist		7				
-Backoffice/support		7				
-Executive officers		7				
-Sales managers		7				
-Users - PC skills						
-Users - Platform						

Platform Automation Project Plan Template (continued)

Project:	Platform Automation System		Project Manager:				
Page:	5		Date Updated:				

Event/Activity	Responsible	Weeks Precedence	Target Begin	Target End	Actual End	Status
-Conduct final review and setup of training site	Project Team	-1				
-Establish/activate training passwords for training lab	Project Team/Users	-5				
-Conduct training:	Project Team					
-Network administration	Project Team	2				
-PC trainer	Project Team	6				
-Training specialists	Project Team	6				
-Backoffice/support	Project Team	4				
-Executive officers	Project Team	4				
-Sales managers	Project Team	3				
-Users - PC skills	Project Team	-2				
-Users - Platform	Project Team	-6				
-Conduct follow-up refresher training	Project Team	-12				
5. Installation/Activation:						
-Install equipment:						
-Physical branch prep	Users/Project Team	3				
-Equipment staging	Hardware Vendor	3				
-Delivery	Hardware Vendor	2				
-Installation	Hardware Vendor	1				
-Testing/Acceptance	Project Team	1				
-Activate platform system:						
-Pilot site test	Project Team	0				
-Branch prep/setup	Users/Project Team	-4				
-Activation of system	Project Team	-6				
G. PROCESS TERMINATION						
1. Postimplementation review	Project Team	-8				
2. Termination	Project Team	-12				

Appendix II

Telephone/Communication Systems Project Plan Template

Telephone/Communication Systems Project Plan Template

Project:	Telephone/Communications Systems	Project Manager:
Page:	1	Date Updated:

Event/Activity	Responsible	Weeks Precit/over	Target Begin	Target End	Actual End	Status
A. NEEDS ANALYSIS						
1. Determine bank communication needs/current system	Project Team	64				
2. Develop existing configuratin/identify communication needs	Project Team/Exec Mgmt	62				
3. Develop preliminary communication plan	Project Team/Exec Mgmt	60				
4. Review/analyze potential selection of outside consultant	Project Team/Exec Mgmt	58				
5. Select telecommunications consultant	Project Team/Exec Mgmt	56				
6. Review existing telephone and data communications systems	Project Team	54				
7. Chart existing telephone/data communiction systems	Project Team	54				
8. Identify key users requiring input	Project Team	52				
9. Set up and conduct interview schedules with key user management	Project Team	52				
B. NETWORK/TELEPHONE HARDWARE DEVELOPMENT						
1. Develop/select communication focus group	Project Team/User Mgmt	52				
2. Develop communication needs based upon urgency	Project Team/User Mgmt	52				
3. Formalize existing communication structure into single document	Project Team	48				
4. Develop strategic telecommunications planning document for future rollout	Project Team/User Mgmt	46				
5. Identify organization for managing ongoing voice/data needs	Executive Management	42				
6. Develop recommendations for: -Telephone -Voice network -Data network	Project Team/User Mgmt	40				

278

Telephone/Communication Systems Project Plan Template (continued)

Project:	Telephone/Communications Systems	Project Manager:
Page:	2	Date Updated:

Event/Activity	Responsible	Weeks Predecessor	Target Begin	Target End	Actual End	Status
C. VENDOR ALTERNATIVES AND ANALYSIS						
1. Develop preliminary list of telephone and network hardware vendors	Project Team	34				
2. Contact vendors and submit RFI and/or vendor presentations	Project Team	33				
3. Conduct vendor or presentations	Project Team	31				
4. Review/analyze RFI and/or presentations and select final vendors	Project Team	30				
5. Prepare RFP	Project Team	28				
6. Submit RFP to vendors	Project Team	26				
7. Schedule/conduct site visits	Project Team	22				
8. Receive/evaluate proposals	Project Team	18				
9. Validate responses and review costs	Project Team	18				
10. Select vendors	Project Team	16				
11. Submit for approval	Project Mgr/Exec Mgmt	15				
12. Contract negotiations	Project Manager	13				
13. Contract execution	Project Mgr/Exec Mgmt	10				
D. SYSTEM DESIGN/DEVELOPMENT						
1. Identify location by location telephone needs	Project Team	40				
2. Determine switchboard/console handling (centralized versus decentralized)	Project Team/User Mgmt	35				
3. Determine communication standards and establish for: voice mail, etc.	Project Team/User Mgmt	35				
4. Determine telephone needs for customer service (ACD)	Project Team/User Mgmt	35				
5. Determine branch to branch connectivity requirements	Project Team/User Mgmt	35				
6. Determine mainframe data communication changes and requirements	Project Team	35				

Telephone/Communication Systems Project Plan Template (continued)

Project:	Telephone/Communications Systems		Project Manager:				
Page:	3		Date Updated:				
Event/Activity		Responsible	Weeks Plan/Forecast	Target Begin	Target End	Actual End	Status
E. IMPLEMENTATION							
1. Conduct startup/preparation:							
-Kickoff meeting		Project Team	20				
-Determine implementation schedule		Project Team	15				
-Cable		Project Team	15				
-Phone		Project Team	15				
-Network		Project Team	13				
-Place system orders		Project Team	8				
-Place network circuit orders		Project Team	8				
-Place network orders		Project Team	15				
-Review equipment needs per site		Project Team/Vendor	12				
-Conduct phone station reviews		Project Team	10				
-Place trunk order and carrier selection		Project Team	1				
-Develop necessary security for voice mail		Project Team	13				
2. Cabling							
-Develop cable provider list		Project Team/Cons.	20				
-Develop cable standards		Project Team/Cons.	18				
-Develop request for proposal		Project Team/Cons.	15				
-Submit request for proposal to cable vendors		Project Team	13				
-Receive/review cable proposals		Project Team/Cons.	9				
-Validate responses and costs		Project Team/Cons.	9				
-Obtain approvals		Project Manager	7				
-Place cable order		Project Manager	5				
-Conduct cabling		Vendor	3				
-Conduct post cable sign off and acceptance		Project Team/Vendor	1				

Telephone/Communication Systems Project Plan Template (continued)

Project:	Telephone/Communications Systems	Project Manager:				
Page:	4	Date Updated:				

Event/Activity	Responsible	Weeks Predecessor	Target Begin	Target End	Actual End	Starting
3. Communication						
-Hold initial checkpoint meeting	Project Mgr/Exec Mgmt	10				
-Hold telephone install expectation meeting	Project Mgr/User Mgrs	2				
-Hold bank checkpoint meeting	Project Mgr/Exec Mgmt	4				
-Hold network install expectation meeting	Project Mgr/User Mgrs	2				
-Hold final checkpoint meeting	Project Mgr/Exec Mgmt	-2				
4. Training						
-Develop training schedule:						
-Pretraining	Project Team/Users	5				
-Hands-on	Project Team/Users	5				
-Refresher	Project Team/Users	5				
-Develop ACD training schedule	Project Team/Users	5				
-Develop E-mail training schedule	Project Team/Users	5				
-Develop console training schedule	Project Team/Users	5				
-Develop maintenance management training schedule	Project Team/Users	5				
-Conduct training:						
-Telephone pretraining	Vendor	2				
-Hands-on	Vendor	1				
-Refresher	Vendor	-4				
-ACD	Vendor	1				
-E-mail	Vendor	1				
-Console	Vendor	1				
-Maintenance/management	Vendor	2				
-Incorporate training video in new hire orientation	Project Team	6				
-Develop user guides for usage	Project Team	8				

Telephone/Communication Systems Project Plan Template (continued)

Project:	Telephone/Communications Systems	Project Manager:
Page:	5	Date Updated:

Event/Activity	Responsible	Weeks Precedence	Target Begin	Target End	Actual End	Status
5. Conduct Installation						
-Telephone						
-System delivery	Manufacturer	5				
-Trunk install	Carrier	3				
-Determine/circulate phone numbers	Vendor	2				
-System testing	Vendor	1				
-System cutover	Vendor	0				
-System acceptance	Project Team/Vendor	-5				
-Network						
-Backbone network installation		6				
-Connection to PBX		1				
-Testing of circuit		1				
-Testing of communication		0				
-Activation/cutover	Project Team/Vendor	5				
-System acceptance						

Telephone/Communuication Systems Project Plan Template (continued)

Project:	Telephone/Communications Systems	Project Manager:					
Page:	6	Date Updated:					
Event/Activity	Responsible	Weeks Precedence	Target Begin	Target End	Actual End	Status
F. PROCESS TERMINATION 1. Conduct postinstallation follow up/review -Review maintenance arrangement adequacy -Change control and execution -Review support structure -Repairs -Moves, adds, changes	Project Team/User Project Team Project Team	-2 -3 -4				
2. Process project termination	Project Team	-6				

283

Appendix III

Mergers Project Plan Template

Mergers Project Plan Template

Project:	Mergers		Project Manager:
Page:	1		Date Updated:

Event/Activity	Responsible	Weeks Precutover	Target Begin	Target End	Actual End	Status
A. DATA PROCESSING ISSUES						
1. Select conversion team	User Management	13				
2. Conduct kickoff meeting	Project Manager	12				
3. Review system differences (setup parameters)	Conversion Team	12				
4. Schedule detailed application subcommittee meetings to discuss differences, between organizations	Conversion Team	11				
5. Conduct application meetings:	Conversion Team	10				
-Deposits						
-Loans						
-Finance						
-EFT						
-Operations						
6. Conduct maintenance of systems	Conversion Team	9				
7. Complete the bank database setup	Conversion Team	9				
8. Develop detailed training schedule	Conversion Team	7				
9. Hold final review of database set up parameters	Conversion Team	6				
10. Receive/review test reports	Conversion Team	4				
11. Make corrections from test report review	Conversion Team	4				
12. Conduct training	Vendor	2				
13. Conduct final sign off of conversion	Conversion Team	1				
14. Switch to live processing	Conversion Team	0				
15. Have follow-up walkthrough	Conversion Team/Users	-1				
16. Terminate project	Conversion Team	-6				
B. MARKETING						
1. Make public announcements	Marketing	12				
2. Stage public communications/marketing campaign	Marketing	12				

Mergers Project Plan Template (continued)

Project:	Mergers	Project Manager:				
Page:	2	Date Updated:				

Event/Activity	Responsible	Weeks Precutover	Target Begin	Target End	Actual End	Status
3. Review services/prices	Conversion Team/Mktg	12				
4. Establish new and revised prices	User Management	11				
5. Prepare/order brochures	Conversion Team	10				
6. Submit for approval	Conversion Team	6				
7. Provide advance notification	Marketing	7				
8. Receive brochures	Conversion Team	2				
9. Implementation	Conversion Team	0				
C. COMMUNICATIONS						
1. Identify departments affected assignments	User Management	12				
2. Identify duplication in staff assignments	User Management	12				
3. Develop recommended changes and restructuring	User Management	11				
4. Submit for approval	User Management	7				
5. Develop detailed communication and restructuring timetable and action plan	User Management	6				
6. Implement plan and conduct restructuring	User Management	0				
7. Hold review/follow-up for continued restructuring	User Management	-10				

287

Index

Function, 23
Functional
   committee members, 33,
      34, 41, 196
   members, 27-28, 157
   project committee mem-
      bers, 30

G

Gantt chart, 47, 65-83, 93,
      97, 121, 128, 134, 143,
      145, 164, 175, 199, 207
   calendar dates, 75-77
   definition/purpose, 65-69
   development/usage, 69-72
   events/activities, 72-74
   recording activities/events,
      130
   template, 130, 131
   timelines, 77-83
Goals, 16
   see Time

H

Hardware, 52
   see Computer, Teller
   development, 206, 209, 237-
      245
   implementation, 127
   installation, 7, 30, 127
   requirement definition, de-
      velopment, 239-240
   vendor, 264
   vendor, request for pro-
      posal, develop-
      ment/submittal, 240-
      241
   vendor lists, development,
      240
Head crashing effect, 155
Host communication, 250

Host interface, development,
      234

I

Implementation, 8, 10, 16,
      31, 35, 38, 53, 59, 63,
      120, 131, 150, 188,
      204, 206, 231
   see Hardware, Live, Plot,
      Postimplementation,
      Project, Software, Tele-
      phone/communication
   committee meetings, 197
   date, 48, 56, 130, 131
   deadlines, 63
   time, 131
Individual responsible, 128,
      130
Information-capture mecha-
      nism, 175
Informative/instructive com-
      munication, 152-153
In-house data processing
      unit, 29
Initial
   bank checkpoint meeting,
      257-258
   presentations, schedule,
      220-222
Installation, 16, 63, 120,
      150, 211-212, 262-265
   see Equipment, Project im-
      plementation
Institutionalized functions, 11
Interdepencies, 96
Interface, *see* Host
Internal
   resources, 9
   system testing, 236
Interviews, 213-214
   findings, 214
Issues
   see New

About The Author

Kent S. Belasco is the Director of Information Systems and Chief Information Officer for First Midwest Bancorp, Inc., a multi-bank holding company based in Naperville, Illinois. He has held numerous management positions in Bank Operations, Project Management and Productivity, as well as serving as a consultant to banks and other financial institutions on earnings improvement.

In addition to his B.A. from Lake Forest College and M.B.A. from Lake Forest Graduate School of Management, Mr. Belasco is a Certified Public Accountant, Certified Financial Planner and a Certified Data Processor. Currently Mr. Belasco is pursuing a doctoral degree (Ed.D.) in Business Education with a concentration in Management Information Systems at Northern Illinois University.

He is also the author of *Bank Productivity* (Bankers Publishing/Probus, 1990), *Earnings Enhancement Handbook for Financial Institutions* (Bankers Publishing/Probus, 1991) and *Analyzing Bank Staffing Levels* (Bankers Publishing/Probus, 1991).